Dually Diagnosed Dually Blessed

From Struggle to Purpose

Coventina Waterhawk

Dedication

To John Hildrith, you were a gentle soul, generous with your time, and gave me sage advice. I wish I could have done the same for you.

To Domenica Ortiz, you blessed my life when I met you at the Santa Rosa event. Your smile lit up every room you entered, and I am grateful for our friendship.

To Randy Fowler, we instantly connected in the most dreaded place on earth. I wish you could have seen the light I was trying to guide you to. Though you were in my life for only a couple of months, your passing left a massive hole in my heart.

And to Melissa Ballard, I am thankful we were roommates while hosting a young people's conference, and you stepped in to help me when you noticed I was overwhelmed.

Acknowledgements

I thank everyone who contributed your story to this book. You have exceeded my expectations, and your bravery to share your truth has brought light into my life. Your light will shine in the lives of those who find themselves reading this book and relating to your experiences. I hope they will utilize your coping methods and find peace in their lives like you. Namasté

Contents

Introduction

In the intricate tapestry of human experience, there exists a population often sidelined yet profoundly significant: those who are dually diagnosed with mental health disorders and substance use challenges. Their journey traverses the tumultuous terrain of inner turmoil and external stigma as they confront the intertwined complexities of addiction and psychological distress. Within the shadows of this duality lie stories of resilience, redemption, and remarkable strength.

This book seeks to illuminate the path of those navigating this intricate landscape, shedding light on the struggles, triumphs, and profound insights accompanying the recovery journey.

As we embark on this exploration, we delve into the depths of human complexity, challenging stereotypes and fostering empathy. Through narratives of courage, vulnerability, and transformation, we invite you to witness the resilience of the human spirit in its rawest form.

This book is not merely a collection of stories but a testament to the power of hope, community, and the unwavering human capacity for healing. It is a call to action, urging us to embrace compassion, break down barriers, and build bridges of understanding. Welcome to a world where duality is not a curse but a catalyst for growth and self-discovery – welcome to the realm of dually diagnosed individuals on the journey of recovery.

Chapter 1

Coventina's Story

As a child, I tried to keep my struggles to myself. I wanted to die when I was seven years old. I started snipping the skin on my wrists with manicuring scissors because it eased the mental and emotional torture I had. I wrote poetry about wanting to die. It helped me get through those moments.

At age eight, I got drunk for the first time at my cousin's wedding. It was magic! I felt free and happy and laughed a lot. I danced erratically during the reception, and my family responded with approval. I could not wait to do it again. A fog came over me, and a feeling of being spaced out reduced the intensity of the suicidal thoughts. Many years later, I discovered that feeling spaced out is dissociation, a trauma response.

I dove into school. I liked school. It kept my mind occupied and lessened the urge to cut myself. Sharing my poetry about wanting to die with my closest friends backfired because they turned their backs on me instead of being supportive. Isolation and loneliness ensued even though many people surrounded me. Music and sports were other ways of coping, and the less time I spent at home, the better off I was.

I hated my family. My older brother, mother, and father seemed to be close, and it appeared my parents loved him more than they loved me. I know today that my perception was way off. My family loved me very much, and they tried their best with me. I was very combative and constantly challenged authority.

In high school, drinking with friends in the marching band was my favorite pastime. Even though I had a happy-go-lucky exterior, I still had tortuous thoughts that told me I would be better off dead. I was becoming addicted to alcohol, unaware of the damage I was causing myself and those around me.

I wanted to be someone else. I would take on a best friend's persona, start laughing like them, and listen to their favorite music to feel wanted and accepted. I acted overly friendly to make up for the feelings of inadequacy. My emotions were all over the place, and when people hurt my feelings, I became so distraught to the point of wanting to end my life. I became a people-pleaser and went out of my way to be accepted. The boys I had a crush on, I would give them candy, believing they would like me, but all they did was pretend to like me to get what they wanted.

I would do any dare for acceptance. For instance, a friend made a T-shirt for me on my sixteenth birthday that said, 'Kiss me, I'm horny' and dared me to wear it, so I went ahead and put it on. Then, while walking down the corridor, a boy who walked by said, "I wouldn't kiss you if someone paid me a million dollars." I was devastated, took the shirt off, and wanted to climb under a rock. I felt like cutting again. I learned through therapy that cutting, suicidal ideation, and the inability to manage emotions were symptoms of borderline personality disorder (BPD).

My first hospitalization was soon after I escaped from an abusive partner. I was so distraught that the feeling of worthlessness overwhelmed my being. With a shattered psyche, I had no sense of identity. My parents allowed me and my two young daughters to live with them.

One day, the intrusive thoughts overwhelmed me yet again, and I had to remove myself from my family. I told my parents I was going to the convenience store. However, once I arrived outside the store, I got on the pay phone and called for help. I drove to the psychiatric hospital and called my parents after being admitted. They were furious.

In the hospital, I thought maybe medications would reduce my symptoms. Still, the psychiatrist told me my symptoms were situational, not chemical. I was so upset that I banged my head against the brick wall outside in the courtyard. The psychiatrist placed me on a 24-hour watch, and I had to sit out in the middle of the community room next to a counselor. I felt invisible because nobody took my suicidal thoughts seriously, especially the psychiatrist.

I talked with another patient, a lady diagnosed with manic-depressive disorder, and I related to her symptoms even though mine were not as often as hers. That is why I asked for medication to help with my symptoms. The lady would speak extremely fast, and her mood was upbeat. Then, right in the middle of a sentence, she would stop abruptly, become catatonic for a moment, and then start to cry. At the time, Lithium was the only effective medication for most people diagnosed with manic-depressive disorder. I was released two weeks after being admitted with no medication or any follow-up counseling. I was released back into the world with no help. So, I tried to smile and be funny, but inside, I wanted to disappear forever.

When I returned to my parents, they told me I had to move out. I was so heartbroken because I felt they punished me for being suicidal. No one believed me. No one would listen to me. I cried out many times to no avail. The days and nights became darker and more depressing. Alcohol, my old friend, became my constant companion. I became dependent on prescription pain medication, and I traveled to different emergency rooms for refills. The medication quieted the unsafe thoughts.

I applied for housing assistance, welfare, and food stamps to help raise my daughters. I was incapable of working, so I depended on other people to help me cope with life. I needed help with everyday chores like vacuuming, washing the dishes, and laundry. All I could do was sit on the couch and watch my friends do all the work. I had no genuine desire to live. The only thing that kept me alive was my daughters. I could not leave them without a mother. I was adopted, so I had always felt abandoned, and I did not want my daughters to feel that way.

When the government assistance was approved, my apartment became a party mecca for anyone who wanted to join. "The more the merrier" was my motto, and others took advantage of my generosity because I did not have healthy boundaries. I could not be left alone. Being preoccupied with other people kept the demons out of my head for the most part. I used pain medication, alcohol, and methamphetamines to achieve balance. Balance without chemicals was unobtainable, and I never felt sane. Insanity appeared to be my middle name. My depressive side was more situational back then, though it seemed. I did not understand that I had a chemical imbalance in my brain and that my symptoms were not my fault.

One night, I wanted to take my life because an old boyfriend who was partying with me ended up in my bed with my babysitter, and I became hysterical. Even though my daughters were in their cribs, I proceeded to take a couple of handfuls of pills, washed them down with some alcohol, and expected to pass out and die in my sleep. When that didn't work, I grabbed a large kitchen knife and started cutting my wrist. My old boyfriend heard me and grabbed the knife from me. I sat on the kitchen floor and sobbed for being such a failure.

Frustration grew by the day, thinking there was no hope in sight. Mentally ill people sometimes behave erratically, and most people think the person suffering is immature, and they walk away. For example, those with PTSD experience triggers and flashbacks. When something or someone reminds them of a past trauma, they react negatively. The trauma response is all others see, and the one suffering is more isolated from those around them. Most people are not willing to go to counseling with their loved ones and learn how they can be helpful and supportive, as well as learn coping skills the entire family can benefit from. It takes patience and love for the person afflicted to feel worthy of the help that is out there.

While under the influence, I was a calm, patient, loving, and caring mother; then, I was abusive while I was sober. I finally called CPS (Child Protective Services) for help. When the police arrived, I begged them to take my daughters. They were in danger of my wrath, and I had no solution to stop. After the officers took them away, I thought about attending a recovery meeting. I attended an AA meeting a few weeks before, where members planted the seed of hope. However, I always needed closure, so I drove to the bar one last time to say goodbye to my friends, believing they would care. I had no intention of drinking. Unaware that alcoholism is cunning, baffling, and powerful, when someone offered me a drink, I accepted. I had no willpower. I vaguely remember driving home. I always drove while intoxicated. It amazes me that I never got into an accident or killed my daughters because they were always in their car seats. When I woke up the following morning, I had a moment of clarity, realizing that I needed to get sober for good. Late that night, I attended my first meeting.

Child Protection Services placed my daughters in separate foster homes, and their father suddenly showed up, wanting custody. After our divorce, he never contacted me or my parents to visit. It was sad to watch my older daughter look out the window every time a car passed, hoping it was her daddy coming to visit. I had supervised visitation and only got to see them for one hour per week. To determine custody, I had to undergo a psychological evaluation, and I was diagnosed with BPD and denied custody. The authorities ordered me to go to parenting classes and counseling. Still, there was no effective therapy for BPD at the time, so I continued to struggle.

The judge granted my ex-husband legal and physical custody, and on Christmas Eve, the girls moved in with him. He awarded me reasonable unsupervised visitation. I visited them as much as I could, but I still had symptoms that did not allow that to happen very often. I was depressed because I missed out on all their firsts: first day at kindergarten, first tooth falling out, first homework assignment, etcetera.

When I had five years of sobriety, I was supposed to pick them up for the weekend. When I arrived, their house was abandoned. I did not know where my daughters were, so the following Monday, I started a legal case to obtain custody, even though I did not know where they were. Luckily, the lawyer I hired could locate them and served my ex-husband's legal papers, which ordered him to attend court with our daughters. Their abandoned house was uninhabitable, and the landlord took several pictures of all the damage and forwarded them to me to present to the judge. As soon as the judge saw the pictures, I was immediately awarded temporary legal and physical custody, and they came home with me. Everyone was in shock, especially me, because I had been deemed an unfit mother when I was newly sober.

Life was hectic back then. My daughters were trying to adjust to a new home, new parenting, new school environment, and developing new friendships. I returned to parenting classes to brush up on previously learned skills.

One day, my older daughter and I were arguing over what she would wear to school. We got into a yelling match when I finally blurted out, "Go on a time-out!" (A time-out was one of the skills I learned in parenting class.) She yelled, "Why don't YOU go on a time-out?" I thought, "That's a great idea," so I showered. I was screaming and sobbing out of frustration and hit the walls. I was so angry. Those intense feelings returned, and I had no control over them. As I exited the bathroom, there was a knock on the door, and my younger daughter opened it. Two police officers stood there, and she asked, "Can I help you?" Stunned, the officer asked if everything was OK because a neighbor had called due to the noise and thought the girls were being abused. My youngest said they sent me on a timeout, and my older one chimed in and ensured they knew that SHE sent me on a timeout. The officers asked if I harmed them in any way, and when they said no, the officers left. I was so embarrassed, ashamed, and humiliated and felt guilty for treating my daughters poorly. My breakdowns were ongoing, and I was so frustrated because I felt like a failure, an unfit mother all over again, and I wondered if I would ever be successful at parenting.

Thankfully, my second husband came into the picture and helped me tremendously. He knew of a type of counseling for my daughters called "Kids are Special," so we started the journey of having a blended family and healing old wounds. I was highly stressed and managed the best I could. I coped better with his help until he started getting ill. He had an autoimmune disease that wreaked havoc on his body, and he was hospitalized several times. We managed to get married between his hospitalizations. My focus was on him and my daughters. I did not have time to focus on myself.

One night, my husband decided to leave. He had made up his mind that using drugs again would alleviate his suffering, and he could end his life on his terms. I could not imagine my life without him. He was my lifeline in so many ways. Distraught, the suicidal thoughts returned. They consumed me, and I couldn't think straight. I needed help. I knew I was in trouble, and I had to try to stay alive for my daughters. The HR manager helped me complete the temporary disability paperwork, and I entered the hospital the next day. My parents helped with my daughters. Once again, I was misdiagnosed with major depression. The psychiatrist said my symptoms were situational, and I was placed on an antidepressant. A couple of days later, a social worker and my parents sat me down and told me that my daughters would live with my parents. So, even though it was not court-ordered, I lost custody of my daughters one more time for being mentally and emotionally unstable.

The night before I entered the hospital, my husband contacted his mother, who contacted me and told me I needed to pick him up at the hospital where he was discharged. I begged her to get him because I was unstable, but she refused, so I picked him up. Our car he drove away in was gone. He wore different clothes and had lost so much weight that I barely recognized him. He covered his left hand, and when I told him I knew he sold his wedding ring for drugs, he started sobbing and apologized. I told him it was OK and that I understood. However, because he was actively using drugs again and wiped out our bank account in two hours, I could no longer trust him, and he needed to move out. I drove him to his mother's house and told her I needed to care for myself. Luckily, she had built a cottage for him in her backyard, so he had a roof over his head and was in a safe place to get sober again.

One week after being discharged from the hospital, I had a manic episode. I assaulted a tow truck driver who had my car attached to his truck. I was so outraged that I kept hitting him, so he called the police, and they came and arrested me. I was in jail for five days, and I almost lost my job because I didn't contact my boss to inform her of my situation. I did call my mother-in-law to check on my husband. She said he was back in the hospital, and this time, he was terminal. He was diagnosed with a rare pneumonia, and his oxygen level was deteriorating.

The day that I was released from jail, I rushed to the hospital. When he saw me enter the room, he turned away and did not want to talk to me. I apologized for kicking him out of the house and told him I still loved him and would be by his side. Four days later, he passed away.

Eight months after his passing, I had another manic episode. I argued with my roommate, and rage took over me. I grabbed one of my dogs and threw her over the balcony. Luckily, a group of kids caught her. I came out of the fog I was in, realized what I had done, and immediately went into the bathroom, took apart a razor, and cut my arm to punish myself for doing such a horrible act. Remember, one of the symptoms of BPD is self-harm. I refused to leave the bathroom, so my roommate called the authorities to help. I was catatonic and did not realize there was blood running down my arm. The police officers eventually lured me out and escorted me to the hospital, where I was finally diagnosed with bipolar disorder and re-diagnosed with BPD. They prescribed Lithium; however, it made me catatonic, and I could not function, so they prescribed something else. In 1993, Marsha M. Linehan, PhD, developed an effective therapy for BPD. It was called DBT (Dialectical Behavior Therapy), and I started learning the tools how to cope with my symptoms. Information about this therapy is in the resources section.

During one hospitalization, my daughters had to visit me on my birthday. I felt horrible. I was responsible for being admitted one more time because I would stop taking the medications. I managed for a while without them, but at some point, I crashed, and one more time, I ended up in the hospital. I was tired of the side effects of the medications and believed I could manage without them.

Fast forward to when I was eighteen years sober. I was hospitalized for thirty days. Suicidal ideation returned because I got fired from a job I loved and could not find another one for weeks. My unemployment benefits ran out, and my roommate evicted me, knowing my mental state, but she did not care. She wanted money. My portion of the household bills accumulated to an unmanageable amount, and I was overwhelmed.

We were going to a women's retreat, and the day before we left, she said, "You don't have a home to come to when the retreat is over." When the retreat was over, two other friends dropped me off at the hospital, and the hospital placed me in the psychiatric unit. I had nowhere to go. I was homeless and hopeless, and again, I felt like it was my fault for ending up there.

I connected with a gentle soul, a man who struggled like me. We promised to keep in touch after we were discharged. Two months after we were discharged, he called me and asked if I could come to be with him. He was distraught, and naturally, I showed up. It was apparent he stopped taking his medications and started smoking marijuana. His friend was there, and he [my friend] acted OK while his friend was present. However, shortly after his friend left us, he became hysterical over his marriage and how he could not envision his life without his wife. All I could do was console him and tell him he would be OK. I made sure he was OK before I left him that night. The next morning, I received a call from the local police department asking me about his demeanor the night before because his friend told them he was OK when he left him with me. They wanted to know what I said to him to upset him. I informed them [police] that he had been upset but was OK when I left. Apparently, he was so distraught that after I left, he turned the stove's gas on and went to sleep, not intending to wake up. However, when he woke up the following morning, out of anger, he lit a match and blew up his apartment and sustained over 60% burns to his body. I was devastated.

Here, I tried to be there and console someone who was inconsolable. I went through the "If only this, if only that" my friend would be OK. If only he stayed on his medications after he was discharged from the hospital. If only his wife would be more supportive. If only he did not start smoking marijuana, he'd be clear-head-ed and stable. He was flown to the burn unit but succumbed to his injuries two weeks later. I started receiving death threats from his family. They were convinced that it was something I said to him that caused him to take his own life. I have been haunted by this experience ever since.

Working full-time was practically impossible, even though I was good at what I did for a living. The longest job I held was three and a half years, and I was hospitalized once during that time. Temporary jobs suited me best because I could only handle a part-time job. Sometimes, I lost a job because of an outburst of some sort when a supervisor instructed me to do something that felt demeaning or disrespectful. I did not know at the time that my reactions were trauma re-sponses.

I was frustrated and felt humiliated, worthless, and unlovable. It felt like all my reactions were due to immaturity and not mental illness. I judged myself and felt judged by others. I felt like I could not keep friendships because I was dam-aged goods. I felt like others would be better off without me, and I would no longer be a burden to them. I felt like my daughters did not need a mentally ill mother around them.

I had a friend who was like a brother to me. One evening, I discovered that my feelings crossed the friendship line. It triggered a severe emotional reaction to those feelings. I felt I could not face him and tell him how I felt. I felt like I was going to die if I expressed my feelings to him, so I kept the mental and emotional torture to myself for months. Once again, the inability to manage my emotions escalated into a PTSD trigger, and it got in the way of our friendship. The intense emotions I felt and the beliefs that I still had (that I was unlovable, undeserving of love, did not have the right to love, and incapable of giving love) were paralyzing me to the point that I could not be around him. I also felt like a liar and a fraud because I told people he was like my brother. When I *was* around him, I acted differently, and one night, he confronted me and asked why I was so 'nutty' around him. I became hysterical, started sobbing, and tried to tell him how I felt, which I was too afraid to say to him because I did not trust that I would be OK. I had known him for a long time. I was his friend through *his* relationships; as I mentioned, he was like a brother to me. I was terrified of losing his friendship if I spoke my truth. I tried to calm down but could not. He responded that he was still my friend, but after he told me everything was OK, I still felt like I was going to die, and the thoughts and feelings were so intense that I started cutting my wrist as soon as I returned home.

I had to stay away from him for quite a while to take care of myself. It took a long time for my emotions to get back to normal. After two long years, I reached out to him. Our friendship is not like it used to be. We rarely speak. I regret my decision to reveal my true feelings. A spiritual counselor advised me never to share my feelings because it would change our friendship forever. She was right.

Today, when I am struggling, I no longer need to hide my pain, and I can be an example of how to live your truth. I continue to do my best to help others with similar challenges. I learned that getting out of myself and living altruistically (an unselfish concern for others) is one of the best antidotes for my mental health.

In December 2001, I attended a tarot class, and the students were assigned a partner to conduct a one-card reading for each other. I was paired with a woman I had met only a week before and knew nothing about her. Once I saw the images on her card, thoughts, feelings, and pictures flooded my mind, and she validated everything I channeled. The teacher and the other students were stunned by my accuracy. It was a challenging time in her life, and I was able to comfort her. I then started doing tarot readings for friends and eventually started conducting tarot readings as a side job.

Returning to the thirty-day hospitalization, a friend allowed me to live with her after I was discharged, and I started working at a casino. However, a couple of months after I moved in with her, her boyfriend started an argument with me and shoved me against the wall. I felt my life was in danger, and I called my parents and asked them if I could return home. I was grateful they said yes. I returned to the safety of their home two days later.

Soon after I returned to my parent's home, I applied for permanent disability for mental health challenges. One section of the application to fill out was the history of my mental health struggles. What I discovered was that I had been hospitalized five times in the last ten years of employment. It was clear that I did not belong in corporate America. Five months later, I received the approval letter. Even though I was grateful, I felt ashamed about being mentally ill. I was thirty-nine years old. When people asked me what I did for work, I lied and said I retired early. Having a 'silent' disability has not been easy because I don't 'look' disabled. There is still a huge stigma surrounding mental health disorders, even though several famous people have come forward recently about their struggles.

A lot has changed since March 2006, when I discovered Reiki. Reiki is a Japanese technique of channeling energy for stress reduction and relaxation, and it also promotes healing of all kinds: physical, mental, emotional, and spiritual. It also can be sent remotely. I believe the combination of Reiki, traditional therapy, EMDR, living the principles of recovery, and applying the coping skills I acquired along the way have kept me from being admitted to a psychiatric hospital for a very long time.

In June 2010, a woman in charge of a health fair contacted me to conduct tarot readings in San Francisco, CA., at Fort Mason for the employees on Saturday, then on Sunday, go to Alcatraz Island to give the employees Reiki. However, the Fort Mason employees enjoyed their reading so much that they told the Alcatraz employees they should ask for a reading. So, I gave each employee a five-minute reading and then five minutes of Reiki. I then started combining the two and lovingly called them "R&R." I occasionally supplement my disability with readings and Reiki. I am mindful of my limitations and don't schedule too many weekly appointments. I need to live a slow-paced life and take time for self-care. Even though it took many years to accept my mental disability, I am grateful I can share my truth at recovery meetings because every time I do, people approach me afterward and thank me for sharing because they, too, are dually diagnosed.

I have acquired a plethora of coping skills throughout my journey, and they are shared in the coping methods chapter. Find the methods that resonate with you. Everyone is different. These methods can also apply to family and friends. Recovery can be for everyone, and using the spiritual (not religious) principles of recovery in our daily lives can create an unshakeable foundation of unconditional love and support where everyone thrives. Gratitude will become the driving force of everyday life, becoming a beacon for others. Darkness will be something of the past. Even though we may sometimes feel down, we no longer get so deep that we cannot climb out. Being honest with ourselves enables us to speak our truth to others confidently. I want people to know that no matter what your diagnosis is or if you're like me and have more than one diagnosis, you can stay sober through it all and live a happy, fulfilling life.

Chapter 2

Diagnoses

I will break down every diagnosis I have the best I can so you can better understand what I go through regularly. If you relate to any of these symptoms, I suggest you find help. The first one is bipolar II disorder. All humans go through ups and downs. It is normal and natural. However, the ups and downs that I go through are anything but ordinary. When I am down, I cannot function, I cannot get out of bed no matter how hard I try, and sometimes I get so low that suicidal ideation returns, and homicidal thoughts infiltrate my mind.

Friends who do not understand say that when they do not want to get out of bed, they force themselves to do so anyway. It is not that I don't *want* to get out of bed; I *cannot* get up. It is as though a large sheet of concrete is on top of me, and the weight almost suffocates me. Or I have no energy but to sit in front of the television for hours and hours.

I can't reach out to others because I feel worthless, and self-pity engulfs me. I never want to be a burden to anyone, not even a therapist or psychiatrist, so I do not use the phone for help. Besides, the phone seems to weigh three thousand pounds, right?

Take today, for example. I was supposed to go grocery shopping and wash my car. I could not even get out of my pajamas, but I continued to write this book, so at least I did something productive.

I also tend to 'eat my feelings' so I gain weight when I am depressed, which causes more depression. It is a vicious cycle. My eating disorder has separate symptoms: obsessing, eating, feeling remorseful, feeling worthless, eating, giving up, thinking, "What's the use?", being preoccupied with food, planning my life around food, inviting friends to go out to eat because it is easier to accept my addiction if other people around me are eating. I cannot abstain from food. It is challenging to start eating healthy foods instead of foods that damage my body.

While manic, I have the energy to exercise, focus on healthy foods, and lose weight. Then, while depressed, I no longer have energy, eat comfort, unhealthy foods, and then gain weight again. Mania is addicting because I feel euphoric, and nothing can stop me from completing tasks that I can't do while depressed. Erratic behavior like spending money I don't have and driving recklessly makes me feel immature because grownups don't behave that way. Then, I remind myself that erratic behavior is a massive part of the mental illnesses I have.

One time, I exited the freeway offramp at eighty miles per hour. I am lucky and grateful that nothing bad happened. Suicidal ideation returned, and when I reached out to my psychiatrist, she suggested I go to the hospital. I had an errand to attend to first; I had to meet with a friend before I went to the hospital. He noticed I was manic, stopped me from getting into my car, and asked what was happening. I talked extremely fast and told him I was going to the hospital but needed to go home to get some clothes. He grabbed my keys and said I wouldn't drive anywhere, so he drove me to the hospital. He saved my life that day. I will never forget that generous act. He saw a friend in trouble, and he took charge.

Ignorance has caused many friendships to fade away. I then get depressed again and feel worthless and that I do not deserve friends in the first place, ad infinitum.

The following disorders I will talk about are BPD and complex PTSD combined. I am combining them because one seems to trigger the other or overlap. Some of the symptoms of BPD are being terrified of being abandoned or left alone and having unstable relationships. Impulsive, self-destructive behaviors, self-harm, extreme emotional swings, and explosive anger are also symptoms that may interfere with daily life. Some of the complex PTSD symptoms include flashbacks, nightmares, behavior changes, avoidance of reminders of the trauma, being easily upset or angry, intrusive thoughts, engaging in risky, reckless, or destructive behavior, and hypervigilance.

**The two diagnoses were several years before seeing an EMDR therapist. Midway through therapy, she said that my symptoms were Complex PTSD and not borderline personality disorder, so I no longer live with the stigma that most people don't understand and judge me for.

When I was seven years old, I was so angry at my mother that I threw my mattress out into the hallway. I screamed at her, "You can't tell me what to do. You're not my real mom!" (I was adopted at six weeks old.)

Being ignored while voicing my thoughts or feelings caused me to react detrimentally to my and others' well-being.

Complex PTSD was the result of surviving torture and unimaginable abuse by a loved one. They held me captive, and they raped me regularly until I escaped. I was in other abusive relationships, and they compounded complex PTSD: nightmares, suicidal ideation, hopelessness, and loneliness ensued. Cutting or eating was the only relief I had.

Being sexually traumatized has been one of the most difficult to recover from. I learned that complex PTSD never goes away, but awareness of trigger responses helps to reduce symptoms while experiencing flashbacks. I must tell myself, "This is not real; it's only a memory, and you are safe." Most people think you can get over complex PTSD and that you are allowing your past to control you, that you have not moved on.

Emotions can be difficult to identify. I could only notice when I was happy or full of rage. There were no middle-of-the-road feelings. You can get an online chart that describes each emotion with a face, so you can practice looking in the mirror until you can label your feelings. The next chapter is devoted to the coping methods that I have used to maintain stability.

Chapter 3

Coping Methods

I have had much therapy throughout the years, and it has helped me get over the hump of wanting to hurt myself. At the beginning of my therapy journey, DBT (Dialectical Behavior Therapy) was the most effective for me because it treats bipolar disorder. Information about how to find help with this type of therapy is in the resources section of this book.

There are several coping skills I have learned over the years, including how to manage my emotions. During a crisis, I can distract my attention and do something else, usually by holding an object or a substance like ice. I learned to be mindful and concentrate on doing one thing at a time. I learned how to act in a way that is opposite to how I feel; if I feel sad, I try to laugh or smile. If I am overwhelmed, I try to take a hot shower or bath or reach out to someone I trust.

One time, I was so distraught that when I called a friend, she told me to shower because she knew it would calm me down. Radical acceptance is another tool I learned. In practical matters, radical acceptance while I am driving looks like this: if someone cuts me off, I get upset at the moment, ask myself, "Did they really have to do that?", then immediately think, "Apparently, otherwise it would have been different" and let it go. It is the same skill that I use when losing a loved one, especially losing someone to suicide. I learned how to be successful in relationships by healthily voicing my needs and wants. When my emotions are intense, I try to snap a rubber band on my wrist; it mimics the sensation of cutting. When my thoughts are overwhelming, I try to think about a friend going through a more challenging time than me and reach out to them and ask how *they* are doing. I like doing soothing things, such as listening to calming music, coloring, or playing games. Hidden objects games are my favorite.

Most people look for someone who is mentally stable and wants the perfect partner. Because of our world, finding someone unaffected by the harsh realities around us is almost impossible. Many people have been traumatized to some extent, whether it is from the loss of a loved one or some dysfunctional relationship. The ways some people cope is by drinking alcohol or doing illicit drugs. Some people rely on retail therapy or turn to food for comfort. Being sober for a long time, I reach out to friends or attend a recovery meeting. Writing in a journal is another coping method that helps me proceed through challenging moments. Sometimes, I feel less than others for needing extra tools to live a healthy, productive life. However, my experiences have allowed me to help others with the same issues. If they do not know where to go for help, I have multiple resources they can use to determine if those specific therapies work for them. Some people feel trapped in their minds and feel no way out of their despair. I am a walking example of the possibilities of therapy, medications, other skills, and supportive friends and family, which can be effective in living a happy, serene life.

Now, about a touchy and controversial topic: medications and the side effects I have endured. Not everyone needs medications to help manage their symptoms. There are other coping skills later in this chapter that others (and I) have used.

Everyone has different brain chemistry and metabolizes medications differently. What works for one may not work for another. Let us look at the first medication the psychiatrist prescribed to me after I was admitted to the hospital when my husband disappeared. I was diagnosed with major depression. The doctors said my symptoms were situational, and they prescribed an antidepressant. However, it caused manic episodes when I was arrested for assaulting the tow truck driver, tossing my dog over the balcony, and cutting my arm.

When I was finally diagnosed with bipolar disorder, the psychiatrist prescribed Lithium. Lithium is supposed to help reduce the severity and frequency of mania and help relieve or prevent depression. However, Lithium caused a severe side effect where I was catatonic and could not function. It usually takes several weeks for a medication to become therapeutic, but I did not have weeks; I only had a few days of temporary disability before returning to work.

The psychiatrist tried administering an anti-seizure medication. He also prescribed an anti-depressant along with an antipsychotic to help me sleep. The combination did stabilize me, but the side effects from the antipsychotic medication caused me to gain sixty pounds, and it ultimately killed my libido.

Mood stabilizers help control mania, antidepressants help relieve depression, and antipsychotics help me sleep. I am by no means a medical professional, and only you and your psychiatrist can determine what medications, if any, are therapeutic for you. I cannot be given an antidepressant without a mood stabilizer; otherwise, I experience mania. I am more on the depressive side of bipolar disorder, so it is challenging to adjust my medications to where they are therapeutic and do not cause hypomania or mania. It has been a long haul and sometimes debilitating trying to manage symptoms during a medication adjustment. Over time, I build up a tolerance because my doctor needs to increase the dosage of the medications or change medications altogether. I'm currently taking medications that have stabilized me for several years, and I am grateful that I have a balanced life and can help others.

One common characteristic of people who take psychiatric medications is that they stop taking them due to the side effects and are impatient with the time it takes for the medications to become therapeutic. At the beginning of taking medications, I often felt fine and thought I could manage without their help, so I stopped taking them. Little did I realize that the reason why I felt fine was because the medications had become therapeutic and stabilized me. Taking or not taking medications or making my adjustments without a doctor's supervision has landed me in the hospital more than I care to admit. One time, I was able to be without medication for nine months until I crashed again and ended up in the hospital. Looking back, I had become addicted to going to the gym and working out at least five days a week. The endorphins kept the depression away, but I would occasionally act out inappropriately being manic.

Meditation and mindfulness are other tools that help me cope. I learned transcendental meditation almost forty years ago. It is the focus on a mantra, one repetitive phrase, or a particular sound. My favorite mantra is, "I am love." Meditation is observing (breathing, feeling, focusing on an object, mantra, or mental picture). Mindfulness is observing what one is doing. For example, while washing my hands, I look at the water coming out of the faucet, what it sounds like, how it feels on my hands, and how the soap feels and smells. I then notice the towel, the color, and how it feels, and I see my hands going from wet to dry. It sounds silly, but when in crisis, it soothes intense emotions, and they become tolerant enough to move forward.

Spending five minutes in the morning and five minutes in the evening on meditation makes a huge difference in our mental and emotional health. Writing a daily gratitude list while going through a challenging time helps manage intense emotions—at least, for me. It helps reduce the intensity of my thoughts and feelings. It also allows you to read what you have written to someone you can trust and be open to receiving a different perspective on your situation.

No matter how minimal, exercise is beneficial to coping with mental health issues, even if it is a five-minute walk. Getting out in nature is very soothing to the soul. I have struggled with this skill, and my weight has fluctuated as a result. As I shared before, I managed well for nine months without medication, but it was from exercising ten hours a week. The endorphins kept me from getting depressed. I was fortunate to have supportive friends with whom I could exercise. It kept me motivated to keep going. I felt I could accomplish anything. I now find that getting restarted is challenging but achievable. Being around water is also soothing, and visiting the beach is calming. When I travel to the beach, I bring my journal and reflect on what is happening in my life. Attending sweat lodges and drum circles are other tools I use. They connect me with the heart of Mother Earth, and I am more grounded than ever. Sound healing (crystal singing bowls, tuning forks, and chimes) also help me release what no longer serves, such as old beliefs, negative self-talk, and inadequacy.

Currently, I use Oracle and tarot cards for daily messages and inspiration. Many spiritual authors share their wisdom through their card decks and books, and my favorites are authors from the publishing company Hay House. The metaphysical and spiritual communities I discovered online enhance my overall well-being, and being unconditionally loved and supported empowers me to live my heart's desires.

The elements of air, fire, water, earth, the moon, and the sun also affect my daily life. Below is a daily invocation I wrote for times of struggle:

I call upon the mighty wings of my feathered friends to lift me with inspiration, hope, and a new understanding of what's to come.

With wind gusts of a powerful tornado sweep away all doubt and fear from my thoughts. Rid me of the distilled beliefs that have kept me in bondage for so long.

I welcome new ideas, wisdom, and beliefs that bring healing and restoration to my mind.

Come, Powers of Air! Bless Me and Be Here Now!

I call upon the mighty volcanoes with their fiery energy to vitalize my Spirit when I feel depleted.

Ignite me and illuminate me for all to see my brightness.

Bring me your vitality, passion, and creativity.

Burn away all negative energy that has transformed into illness and let me rid the ashes forever.

Come, Powers of Fire! Bless Me and Be Here Now!

I call upon the mighty oceans for their cleansing, to crush my sorrows, grief, and painful emotions with their powerful waves, allowing them to go out with the tides.

Bring me peace and serenity like the stilled ponds. Help me fall in love with my reflection as I see myself for who I truly am.

Let my gratitude and joy flow out of me like the incredible rushing waterfalls and help me receive and give compassion as I heal.

Come, Powers of Water! Bless Me and Be Here Now!

I call upon the mighty mountains to bring the physical strength I need to heal my broken body.

I ask for sustenance, grounding, and time to rest upon my mother's belly.

Reveal the ancient wisdom within me as I utilize the sacred plants and herbs to my advantage during restoration.

Allow me to receive your abundance with grace and dignity.

Come, Powers of Earth! Bless Me and Be Here Now!

I call upon the mighty Spirits of all life for help, healing, and restoration.

Strengthening the bonds of love and trust and open my mind to every kind of healing possible.

Whether it be the stars, planets, winds, waters, plants, human touch, or prayers.

Allow it all to come into every fiber of my existence, for I ask for total change and transformation.

Come, Powers of Center! Bless Me and Be Here Now!

By the Air that is Her Breath,
The Fire of Her bright Spirit,
Waters of Her Living Womb,
and the Earth that is Her Body,

I cast a protective circle around me throughout this day.

Blessed Be!

Figuring out what coping skills work best for you is a journey of self-discovery, acceptance, healing, and self-love. If I can find stability with mental illness and long-term recovery to the point of not having suicidal ideation for many years and no relapse, so can you. Hang in there. It gets better.

The following chapter contains personal stories of others who also have substance use disorders and mental health challenges, and they share their experiences and coping skills that have enabled them to live a stable, happy life. We hope you find comfort in knowing you are not the only one who sometimes suffers.

Chapter 4

Personal Stories

Ashley's message to Postpartum Anxiety and Postpartum Depression

I had postpartum anxiety and did not even realize it till a year or so later. I did not have it this bad, but it was scary. I cried a lot and had a ton of other things going on. I am writing to remind you that if you know someone who has had a baby in the last year, ask THEM how they are doing. Please do not go straight for the baby. If anything, go help Mama during the first couple of visits—food, cleaning, laundry. PPD and anxiety can be severe, so please be open-minded and know they might need help. Here are the thoughts of one Mama on her PPD:

"Dear postpartum depression and anxiety, F*** you. No really. F*** you. You have ruined so much for me. You have tortured and tormented me to the brink of my existence. Because of you, I am constantly in pain. Because of you, I feel lost, hopeless, unwanted, rejected, hateful, neglected, angry, frustrated, stupid, crazy, and unloved. Because of you, I have found that, at times, I could not enjoy being a mommy and looking at my beautiful baby. You and you alone made me feel like I was not good enough. You taught me that I do not matter. You showed me that no one cares about me. It bothers me that you didn't listen to a word I said. And it bothers me that you didn't care about who you hurt or who you made me hurt. My exhaustion allowed you to hone in on every insecurity I've ever had and made me feel completely insignificant.

Because of you, I missed out on some of the most critical moments of my baby's life. Because of you, I have felt like I did not deserve to live another moment, take another breath, or speak another word. Because of you, I am constantly in agonizing pain, and I do not know how to make it stop, and I no longer care about pain.

You made me forget what day it was to shower, eat, sleep, and do basic things people should be doing. You made my friends ignore me because no one wants to be around someone who's always negative. You made a massive hole in my heart, and you made me not give a damn about it. You made me fearful for anyone I knew was going to have a baby, terrified they would suffer with this pain, too.

You caused me great suffering, and I have no way to punch you in the face for some relief. You caused me to binge until I vomited because I had not eaten in days, and I did not know how to stop. You caused me to distance myself from my family because I think you are a contagious disease, and I do not want them to feel this way.

You took everything from me. You took my willpower to live, my faith in myself, and even my ability to breathe. You took my happiness and created my hell just because you wanted to because you felt like it. You demolished my outlook on life and caused me to lose hope completely.

You did this. You made me feel this way. Because of you, I hate being around people now and want to hide. Because of you, I hide in the bathroom and cry for hours in the middle of the night so no one hears me and asks what is wrong.

Because of you, I wanted to die. Because of you, I have thought of driving into oncoming traffic, taking a bunch of pills and which ones to take, jumping off bridges, drinking antifreeze, and a variety of other methods to satisfy your hunger for my pain and hunger for release from you. I do not want to die. I want to enjoy my baby, clean my house, take showers, do laundry, do my makeup, cook, eat, and do everything else an average person would want to do. But because of you, I cannot. I am immobilized because I am in your grasp. You have a hold on me that I cannot break from. I hate you.

I want people to STOP saying I am crazy. I am not crazy; I'm in f***ing pain! I want people to LEARN about this horrible DISEASE they say is "all in my mind," and "you're just making it up," or "you just want attention," "It's not that bad," and "Everyone gets baby blues," "It's not real," "Talk to God about it" and "Women have been having babies for tens of thousands of years, and they got through new motherhood just fine." and "Toughen up." and "Yeah, I had a few bad days there after my baby was born. I know what you are going through." and "I just finished my [album/thesis/marathon/political campaign/essay]. I know how you feel." and "Maybe postpartum depression is God's way of letting you know you do not have enough faith. I think you should pray harder." And "Stop making this about you. Your focus should be on your baby. You should be thinking about them rather than yourself." "I would never take antidepressants. You should not need that stuff to be a mother." and "You're just mad the baby is getting all the attention." and "PPD is just a fad. Only spoiled women get it, and now that it is "popular" everyone is jumping on the bandwagon." and "Can't you see how lucky you are? You have a beautiful baby! You should be grateful" and "You're just using postpartum depression as an excuse to get out of the hard work of being a mom." and "Once you go back to work, you'll probably feel fine." And "Why can't you just talk yourself out of this? I do not think you're trying hard enough." and "Do we need to take your child away from you?" and "If you would just try _____(fill in the blank) parenting style I think everything would be OK." and "You have [a supportive partner/wonderful home/great family/good job/food on the table/healthy baby]. You should be happy." and "All of this crying is bad for your baby, you know." and "We all have days where we don't want to get out of bed." And "Did you think motherhood was going to be easy? What did you expect?"

NEWS FLASH: we do not f***ing want to feel this way. I'm not seeking attention, which doesn't mean we don't deserve our kids! STOP MOM SHAMING US! We are hurting. And in pain, this is not a f***ing fad or make-believe. It has been around forever; even animals can get PPD/PPA/PPP. My cat had it after she lost two litters of kittens. So, no, it is not f***ing make-believe, and no, we don't want it, and no, we can't just f***ing get over it.

If you have made it this far, thank you. Thank you for caring enough to discover what's on my mind and what's been happening to me. I can say I do not feel anywhere near as horrible as I used to, so I've expressed feelings here that I have overcome, but I wanted you to see exactly how bad this was for me at different points in trying to deal with this pain. I want you to under-stand the severity of what some people suffer from. And I want you to know that compared to some, my case is MILD. How f***ing scary is that? This writing was inspired by me reading another woman's PPD letter. Her letter is much more uplifting than mine and was directed to women with PPD to read and feel inspired not to give up. Mine is dark because I want to encourage people to learn what the f*** they're talking about, and maybe, just maybe, someone will be able to get help, and perhaps someone will learn to understand.

Share if you like, but these are my words, and they are from the deepest part of my heart and soul. Please help others understand that we who suffer do not wish to; it is accurate and not something we can control."

Jess's Story

I have struggled on and off my whole life with chemically based severe depression and anxiety. People usually do not want to discuss this topic because they are embarrassed or fearful. There is a taboo in our society about mental health. The brain is the most critical organ in our body. Yet, nobody wants to discuss whether that organ has problems or does not operate perfectly.

I have been one of those people. I have hidden my mental health issues and gone underground until very recently. I would go off Facebook for months or years at a time because I did not want to be accountable to people about what my mental health issues were. I turned off my phone. I was not a part of life for almost three years. I am sharing this not for pity, not for people to ask, "How are you doing?" But for other people to feel like it is safe and OK to talk about their mental health. Talk to a professional, to a friend, to your family.

This past June, with the help of Kaiser Hospital, a few of my doctors finally figured out the right cocktail of medications. I am very pro-western medicine even though I studied Eastern/Chinese medicine. I think both therapies hold a significant place in health care. I always knew that my depression was chemical. I am not angry that it took this long to get the right combination of medication. I am nothing but grateful. I am positive it is chemical because it was like turning on a light switch when Kaiser finally got it right. My life was completely different overnight.

I have gained nearly ninety pounds in the three years since moving here. Some of it was due to the side effects of medication, but most of it was due to me not caring about it and eating all the wrong things. Some of you may have noticed that I now post many photos of the healthy stuff I eat.

It is not an extensive diet. All I started to do was eat lean protein, unlimited vegetables, and unlimited fruit. Whenever I'm hungry, I eat a hard-boiled egg instead of Doritos or some other carbohydrate-heavy snack. I had been living off cheeseburger happy meals from McDonald's. I have lost twenty-two pounds since the end of July. I did not let anyone take photos of me.

My family went on a vacation to San Diego at the end of July, and we had pictures taken. I am very grateful to have these photos; however, I was shocked by my appearance. I know that looks are not everything. But my health suffered from weight gain, and to be honest, I missed my foxy self. My fantastic husband, Kory D. Lee, has not said anything mean or harmful to me during these three years. He has always said that I am beautiful at any weight or mood. He has been taking care of me. He has seen me at my worst. He worked two jobs to provide for our family. We have seen the "For worse" side of marriage, and now we are on the trajectory of being able to see the "For better." For those who know Kory, you know what a genuinely giving, thoughtful, selfless person looks like. He is the definition of all these things.

Since late July, I have been controlling my weight; I have gotten back on Facebook and connected again with some friends and family I had not talked to in a long while. I started my own business and have become a much better wife, daughter, friend, and cat mom.

I could not be the person that I am today without the love and support of Caryn Pola, Bob Pola, Cheri Crafton Neiman, Jeff Neiman, Michelle Carsner, Tiffany Bailey, Carrie Lawrence, Beverly Ulis, Monique Cardinaux, Monika Kroupova-Willenbrink, Shelley Rubenstein, Cass Snyder, Roger Lee, Dorothy Farnandez-Lee, Diane Hume, Kaiser Woodland Hills, and my four cats.

I am forgetting people, but this is not the Academy Awards.

I must thank myself the most for not giving up when things felt hopeless and trusting Kory D Lee when he said things would improve. For being willing to try countless different medications with terrible side effects in the hope of feeling better. For having to withdraw from said medications when it was clear they were not the right ones, for taking my medications every single day. (Half the battle with mental health patients is simply adhering to medication protocols). For believing that I am OK and perfect for who I am. All of this has been hard work.

And the journey continues...

Esther's Life with Anxiety

Anxiety is complicated and often misunderstood. One of the main reasons is that the symptoms appear to resemble other disorders, such as bipolar disorder or depression. Anxiety is several disorders at once. I will share a few of my experiences and give examples of how the disorders overlap.

One of my first forms of anxiety is "Photophobia." Photophobia is the sensitivity to light. About thirty-five years ago, when most stores started using fluorescent lighting, I noticed that I got dizzy every time I went shopping, whether at the grocery store or the mall. I was at the age of youthful raging hormones, so the doctor misdiagnosed it as anemia. It wasn't until recently that I decided to do my research.

I noticed that the symptoms explain what I have been experiencing for the past thirty-plus years. Specific lighting triggers panic attacks. I get dizzy, short of breath, and feel fatigued. Some people with photophobia experience migraines. I am fortunate not to.

Here is an example of where disorders overlap: crowded places also trigger panic attacks, called "Agoraphobia." Often, a store or a crowded mall triggers both disorders. At this point, the only remedy for me is to get fresh air. The need for fresh air causes a misunderstanding. People think that I'm "Claustrophobic." Anxiety is very complicated. While driving, if there is any sunshine, I need to wear sunglasses or put down the front visor. (I almost always drive with the visor down). Headlights or a glare from the sun will trigger a panic attack. I will get dizzy and have an elevated heartbeat. Again, fresh air helps, so even if it's twenty degrees and snowing, I roll down the windows. Music also helps me relax. I always drive with the music on. When I have a panic attack, I turn the volume up. I usually get lost in the music and calm down.

Another anxiety disorder is called "Sensory Processing Sensitivity." It is when a person goes into a place where a lot is happening, and their circuits are overloaded. All the activity around them triggers a panic attack. Occasionally, I experience this, but unfortunately, my daughter does experience this symptom quite often.

My daughter has a psychology degree from San Jose State University and now teaches mindfulness to elementary school children in the San Francisco Bay area. We live in a chaotic world. I am grateful that my daughter's private school has implemented a wellness program. At least the children attending her school will be given tools to help them in stressful situations. My daughter's experiences have helped her become an educated and compassionate teacher for our youth. Her education has helped me as well. It is so awesome to learn from our adult children! The basic form of anxiety which most people have experienced from time to time is stress. We all react differently. Some people need to be around others, some need affection, some need to be left alone, and sometimes, it is a combination of both, depending on the timing and situation.

For several years, I have been experiencing family illness/death, bankruptcy, and loss of several homes, and I almost had a nervous breakdown. Although I have my emotions under control, I am constantly tense and on edge. Since I am always on edge, the slightest thing will trigger a panic attack. I pass on get-togethers because my focus right now is on unwinding, and the primary form of anxiety overlaps with another disorder, depression. People see that I pass on activities, am often alone, and think that I am depressed. It is the opposite. I am so wound up that the best way for me to stay calm without medication is by being alone with nature or listening to music.

As I shared before, anxiety is highly complicated, and several disorders can overlap. Solutions are not universal. Everyone is different. Their reasons, reactions, and solutions may vary depending on the situation. In this fast-paced world we live in today, we lack compassion. On the surface, people do not know what another person is going through. Before we ridicule, let us try to accept. The first step is to stay calm and not condemn. I have been ridiculed so many times by people who do not understand. The harsh words are remembered for a lifetime and affect our self-esteem.

When a person is experiencing a form of anxiety or panic attack, they need calm surroundings. Even during a panic attack, a person is not capable of saying "Yes or no" or making a nod of the head. Please keep it simple. Please do NOT ask them what is wrong! It will trigger more anxiety. Ask them if you want to step outside with them to get some fresh air. The answer will be a simple yes or no. If the answer is no, do not ask, "Are you sure?" Say, "Let me know if you change your mind." If you are near water, ask them if they want a glass of water. Sometimes, the simple task of drinking water gets their mind off the anxiety. Again, if they say no, do not ask, "Are you sure?" Say, "Let me know if you change your mind." We may never understand what another is going through, but we can always be compassionate with one another.

Betty's Life with Bipolar II Disorder, Bulimia, and PTSD

My favorite song from when I was little was "Lonely Little Petunia." Some of the words go like this: "I'm a lonely little petunia in an onion patch, and all I do is cry all day."

I was abused and hit a lot because I was always doing things wrong. Once, I climbed up on the roof when I was not supposed to. It was fantastic to see everything from high above everything else. My mom hit me with a belt, and I remember the maids were laughing.

I remember visiting my grandmother and sitting on a rock when I was twelve. Everything seemed "flat," which was depression. From then on, the only times I felt happy were when I drank alcohol, ate sugar, drank caffeine, or was in a loving relationship.

When I arrived at college, I became bulimic, and it gave me relief from the intense emotions. Still, it then caused shame, remorse, and isolation, thinking I was the only one.

I felt inadequate because of my upbringing when I transferred to another college. I was diagnosed with a thyroid problem and prescribed medication, which caused me to gain weight and caused the bulimia to get worse. Then the doctor prescribed diet pills to control my hunger, but they made me wired and full of energy, and my mind raced uncontrollably. One time, I had a psychotic break and shaved my head with a razor. Then I returned to the doctor, and she gave me tranquilizers to calm me down. Still, I felt different and isolated again, even though people were around me.

I did not drink in college until I met my husband, and the alcohol made it easier to vomit, so I continued to suffer from bulimia. I would do whatever I could to cause me to throw up, including putting a hanger down my throat, which caused damage to my esophagus. My emotions were out of control, and the bulimia made me feel in control, and if I felt "full," I felt out of control. The minute I sought help for the bulimia, it stopped, which was a miracle.

I was smoking cigarettes that helped with the weight and suppressed my depressing emotions. When my mother passed away, I got involved with someone abusive, and the mania lasted three years. My behavior was nonstop energy, driving fast, talking fast, and being addicted to the relationship. Then, I crashed and became severely suicidal.

I attended a support group in which one lady suggested I stop drinking, so I did. I went to therapy, and the counselor suggested I go to a psychiatrist because she believed I was depressed. The doctor prescribed Lithium. It first caused me to become manic, but the doctor gave me different types of medication, and the most therapeutic one was the generic timed release, and it has helped ever since. The only side effect is that it has controlled my happy emotions, so I do not get excited during celebrations. However, I do get depressed at times.

I need to exercise every day because it activates endorphins and alleviates depression. I am better now, and I can detect my emotions getting low. I go for a twenty-minute walk, and I instantly feel better.

My father was untreated bipolar, my brother was bipolar, and my great-grandmother was probably bipolar II; she did not want to travel with the family and always looked miserable.

Some of my coping skills over the years have been cooking, walking, swimming, babysitting my grandchildren, having weekly family dinners, and arranging flowers. I also see my psychiatrist once a month and a therapist once a week to help manage PTSD with EMDR therapy (**E**ye **M**ovement **D**esensitization and **R**eprocessing), which allows me to face things that I get emotional about. Having a dog has helped my emotional state as well. I also went into recovery for alcohol and codependency. It has tremendously helped because I find others who think, feel, and sometimes act like I do and do not feel as crazy. I need a creative outlet that makes me feel good, like gardening. If you tackle one thing at a time, you will not get overwhelmed and experience relief.

Laura Writes

"To the man whose partner has anxiety: You might have heard that she has anxiety from sitting by her side in a doctor's office, holding her hands while the tears stream down her face. You might have seen her get angry and explode because she is overwhelmed. Wondering where this rage has come from. You might have seen her sit quietly, staring into the distance with panic in her eyes. You might have guessed, or she might have told you, but either way, there are things you should know.

Anxiety is not a one-size-fits-all; it is not consistent, and it is not always easy to tell. You might think your partner has just snapped at you, but it was anxiety that did it; you might think she is angry, but it is the anxiety that's got a chokehold. You might think she's not enjoying herself when you go out, and it's your fault, but it's not. It is anxiety. You know how she cannot understand when she asks what you think. Why would you respond with "nothing"? It is because she never thinks anything. Her thoughts replay like a freight train in her head full steam ahead, over and over. It is exhausting for her. It is why she is tired.

Not a day goes by without her thinking. She thinks about everything, and usually, it is the worst-case scenario. She worries that something will go wrong; that some days, if she leaves the house, something terrible will happen, like kidnappings, deaths, falls, or cars spinning out of control. That is why she cannot just leave the house or just go out, even though you have suggested it with good intentions.

But it takes work. That is why when your partner is home alone or out by herself, she will text you a million times, tell you her every move, or tell you everything that is going wrong; she knows you can't change anything, she knows you feel helpless, and she knows why she needs to share it with you. Otherwise, her head will explode with panic.

Sometimes, she wonders why you are with her, and if you knew she had anxiety, would you still be there? Do you regret being with her? Do you wish you were with someone else who did not have this vice around their neck? I want you to know I see that this is tough on you, demanding to see your loved one hurt; the pressure for you would be immense. But do not think for a minute that your partner does not see you; do not think for a second that she does not worry about you, too. She even gets anxious about you. She knows it is not your fault, and you want to fix her, but she is whole.

But you can help her; you can loosen the vice. You can see what gets too much for her, the crowds of people or bedtime, dinnertime; see it and help her by holding her hand and telling her you are with her. Do it with her, take over, and ask her to sit down and breathe.

If you see her struggling with appointments, reschedule them and encourage her to take them slowly. Too much is overwhelming for her, even though she has good intentions. Please do not make her feel bad about missing an appointment, a party, or whatever. She wanted to go, but she could not. She already feels bad. Tell her it is OK. Take the kids out for a play. When you see her struggling, encourage her to take time out for herself. If the kids are awake all night and she is worse, get up with her and take over if she has less sleep. Tell her to go back to bed.

Sometimes, the answer will be obscure. Sometimes, your partner will not even know what she needs, but so long as you are patient with her, she will feel your love. She or you will not benefit if you get frustrated; it will escalate and make you both miserable. She does not want her anxiety to define your relationship, and when you are patient, you are telling her you are willing to do the same.

Anxiety is heartbreaking for her. It is. She wishes she could feel free. The free feeling of just being carefree and not a prisoner to this ugly illness. Free of the voice that follows her, listing all her insecurities.

Celebrate the challenging days because she needs them. She appreciates you, and she loves you. She is vulnerable and scared. But she chose you to share her heart's most significant, profound scar tissue. She knew the day she met you that you were worthy enough to see her in all her imperfections. She will love you with her whole heart, and you know she will because she has already listed the pros and cons, and just as you are by her side, she will be fiercely loyal to you. Forever and ever, you need to take her hand and tell her, "I am with you." Love, A woman and a momma who has anxiety."

Ken's Message to a Friend who was Suicidal

FYI. If you are feeling down, at the end of your rope, suicidal, hurt, disappointed by the world, knowing deep down in your heart and soul and mind that this is the end and there is no hope, and nothing will ever get better, do me a favor and hold onto that feeling. Because even though it may suck now, the memory of that terrible vulnerable horrible moment is going to help many people when it happens to them, too. The story of your victory over despair is the greatest gift you can give someone, so never forget, and please know that you are loved, and others will someday need that love in return.

Cathyann's Thoughts

Life on the Border is a matter of disguise of forced smiles and silent sobbing at inopportune moments

There is no answer to why: why is there a burning in my heart,

Why can I only sit and stare,

Why can I only speak in a whisper,

Why is sound overwhelming,

Why will I shatter if you hold me? Just hold me without words.

Carlos Shares

I have always felt different, felt less than. It started with my family. I am the oldest of six children. My father is an alcoholic, and I witnessed him abuse my mother. He would threaten to hurt me as well if I got out of bed. My father left us when I was five years old. When he left, my mother said I was the "man" of the house, so I grew up at that moment, being a surrogate father and husband.

So, the drive was to please people and be perfect. Soon, depression followed. Other things that made me feel less than others were not having a father and being from a broken home. One day, I noticed my skin was brown, being Mexican American, which also made me feel less than. I had the association of being a "lazy Mexican." We were on welfare, isolating me from others. I was an extremely quiet kid and tried to be good. My mother said that because I was the oldest, I had to be an example of being good, and there sprouted my perfectionism. It soon led to depression. Much fear engulfed me.

When I was getting older, I realized things would get worse and not better. I started smoking pot and drinking at age sixteen, and it helped my depression and loneliness. I felt better, my sense of humor came out, and I felt positive under the influence.

During college, I started developing agoraphobia, anxiety, and panic attacks. Because I did not know what was happening, I became depressed, to the point of being housebound for about one month. The only way I could leave was if I had alcohol with me. My friends commented on my drinking, and I sought out help with counseling and saw a therapist, who asked me why I was there, and I said that I felt I had drunk too much. I drank because I was bored and lonely. He asked me if I was an alcoholic, and I said no. I continued to see him while hungover, and he finally suggested I try to stop drinking for one month, so I did to prove that I did not have a problem. I successfully stopped for a month and got drunk to celebrate.

Eventually, the therapist told me I was an alcoholic, and I started crying and told him if he would help me with my loneliness and boredom, I would not drink so much, but he said he could not help me until I stopped drinking. So, he proceeded to bring the phone into the office, opened the Yellow Pages, found the number to Alcoholics Anonymous, and told me to call that number, which I did.

At ten years sober, I could not get to San Francisco for a large get-together that furthered my depression, which led to a thirty-day recovery center. They diagnosed me as depressed and prescribed Prozac, which did not agree with me, so they put me on something else. I have been on so many medications over the years that I cannot even begin to list them here. I am currently taking Zoloft and Abilify, and I have been stable for a long time now.

They said my depression was secondary to agoraphobia, and if I took care of it, I would not be so depressed. They also recommended that I quit my job and go on disability. That started me on the path of therapy, support groups, and working on phobias. I also have PTSD from witnessing my father abuse my mother. I was also traumatized by my cousin and uncle when I was seven or eight years old. That was when people-pleasing became a life skill because I wanted to be liked by others. People pleasing turned into "Dependent Personality Disorder" (DPD), and I need to have someone with a more assertive personality to take charge of the relationship. I draw upon their positive energy to keep me going, and they need to initiate contact; otherwise, I will stay home alone and not socialize with others.

I still have depression and phobias, but I can cope much better with the therapy and medications. I am now working part-time. I started traveling short distances at first and slowly going further and further away from home until I was eventually able to travel to Japan.

Even though I have been married for twenty-nine years, I still get bored and lonely sometimes, so I reach out to my friends.

Steve Suggests

If you suffer from any emotional well-being condition, please consider exercise as part of your treatment. It has been a game-changer for me. It sucked a** at the beginning, and I have had my struggles with diet and consistency, but it helps with my mood.

Depression is a tricky thing-- you can be one inch below the surface of the water and think there is just no hope of getting your head above it all the way and onto the shore. Exercise gives me at least 10 inches, so my head is always at least a little bit out of the water (mostly), and it really helps me not go down the road of despair, which is like a vacuum at times. It is not the cure for me but an essential ingredient, perhaps even vital.

One therapist's experience of being a mental health professional and having mental health issues

The Dirty Little Secret: Professional Stigma in Mental Health by Dr. Anyone (This could be you)

I asked to write a submission describing my coping skills as a mental health professional. I cannot write this without noting that even with my own "woke-ness" around the topic, I still find it difficult to discuss honestly, hence the title "The Dirty Little Secret," as no matter how extricating stigma is discussed, mental health professionals still struggle with deep-seated, internalized criticism of themselves. Even me. Even with many years of recovery from both substance abuse issues and mental health. Still, I'm not too fond of it. I would still rather have any other problem than this. So, here is the first truth I have come to accept:

Stigma is real. It still is pervasive in the industry. And it is a fine line to negotiate as someone who struggles with symptoms. I also believe it is a very private matter and that mental health professionals deserve the same level of privacy as anyone else. Recently, there has been a movement towards "coming out" as a mental health professional with mental health issues. The problem with mental illness is that when you "come out," it's not like cancer; you can't say, "I had this problem, and now I'm forever cured." Most know there is no cure; we are just OK now. And for many of us, we do not know how long "right now" is going to last, how long the meds are going to work, and if we are ever going to spiral down into one of those dark places again. It is a very vulnerable place to be, especially in our professional lives, and most of us are masters of operating like everything is fine. Here is the second most important truth that someone told me:

Every mental health professional needs somewhere where they can be 100% real and vulnerable. Where they can just be 100% honest and not worry about judgment, therapy is usually done with a therapist, but not always. I have developed long-standing relationships with colleagues who joke about things like "You know, it's just that little B-Line "borderline" problem I have" or validate who you are when you are not at your best. Here is my next bit of wisdom:

Self-disclosure is a personal choice. No one should feel any pressure to disclose personally or professionally. In 12-step recovery, the principle of anonymity suggests that recovery is a private matter and should not be shared unless it might help someone. Mental health issues are slightly more complicated even in the 12-step community, where there is continued stigma around mental health, confusion about what it is, and a pervasive faulty belief that the program itself is the solution.

My personal and professional opinion is that in recovery, without the shroud of substances masking underlying issues, many people (not all) have other issues that need to be addressed. Unfortunately, help is challenging to get, as even in the mental health field, many professionals do not understand what they are looking at, which leads me to the following truth:

Being in recovery or being a trained mental health professional does not mean you understand what is going on with you. In fact, we often cannot see what is happening to us. I resisted having any mental health issues at all costs. I had family members with mental health issues, substance abuse issues, workaholism, codependency, and anger problems. My solution to these issues was to do anything to try to be "normal," and the last thing I ever wanted was a mental health issue.

As a young person, I was profoundly depressed. I had my first overdose, albeit on aspirin, in 5th grade. If it was Tylenol, I could have died. I woke up with my hearing impaired and a head that felt full of cotton.

Soon, I began drinking and using drugs, and my family kept trying to tell the professionals that I had a mental health issue. I could see at that point that my lifestyle was the issue, and I felt sure that if I chose not to use substances, these other symptoms would go away. At twenty-one, I hit bottom and got sober in AA. I spent five straight years only doing recovery and barely holding on. I knew my sanity was marginal, but so was the sanity of everyone I knew. People would call me, and even after years of recovery, I would say, "I just feel like dying," and they would laugh and not know what to say. I could NOT accept that there was any other issue except that maybe I needed a new sponsor, a new boyfriend, a new program, more steps, or a new job. It was beyond my wildest dreams that I could have a problem with depression because I could see all the "situational" issues contributing to my problems.

Over the years, my life ebbed and flowed. Things improved because I was just more stable overall. I continued to be active in 12-step recovery, where I always had an outlet for my feelings and a "solution" by working the steps, talking, helping others, and having a spiritual connection to something bigger than me. I practiced every program in the 12-step program continuum: AA, NA, Coda, Al-Anon, Overeaters Anonymous, Food Addicts Anonymous, Debtors Anonymous, and Naranon.

I had a successful private practice and would get depressed from time to time. Still, I had enough support with 12-step recovery that there was always a framework to describe what was wrong and enough of a band-aid to get me relief from socially acceptable crisis to crisis.

Through working in mental health as a psychiatric emergency worker, the desire to ever kill myself or ask for help began to dissipate as I was on the receiving end of people who either were suicidal or from incomplete suicides for evaluation. I saw women come in suiciding over relationships, people coming in not being able to take control of their financial situation, relationships, home life, and substance abuse problems or mental illness. I watched them get help. I saw them get better. I helped them. Which brings me to the following truth:

It is hard to believe that you can still have a problem when you are functioning, and you can do so much good in the world. Because of a promise I had made to a therapist, I agreed to go to see a psychiatrist. You would think, with my background in psychopharmacology and psychotherapy, I would welcome the help, but no, I had more judgment about psychiatry than anyone I knew. I thought my level of depression and anxiety were just situational and that I did not have a severe issue.

To this day, I am so grateful that I followed through with this decision. The psychiatrist asked me in her amiable southern accent, "Well, how often would you say you cry?" I thought to myself, what would sound normal? I decided that once or twice a week sounded normal, even though it was probably once or twice a day. Besides, I had good reasons to cry. I was a sensitive, empathic person. So, I told her, "I probably cry about once or twice a week." She replied, "You know that's not normal, right?" I did not admit it, but I did think that once or twice a week was normal, and in addition, I thought that if my clients cried frequently, it was normal. Certainly, crying in 12-step recovery was expected, or so I thought. But really, it is not. She kindly said to me, "Look, I think you're probably much more depressed than you think, and you've probably been depressed for a long time, so you can't see it." I agreed to give the treatment she suggested a try for one full year.

In that year, I also discovered that I had several blows to the head that were not inconsequential and that I probably had suffered a mild brain injury or concussion, which led to my academic problems and severe decline in 8th grade, not drug and alcohol use.

I began accepting treatment, and we worked on finding the proper treatment regimen for me. We finally found medications that addressed all my issues, and I could not believe how much my life had improved. Through this time, my psychiatrist began to help me understand how many people experience 65-75% recovery, and they never know that there is 25-35% more help available that would make a significant difference in their lives.

We began to talk about the concept of 100% recovery from mental health issues, which I support and believe in today. In the beginning, I wouldn't say I liked the idea of taking medication. I was so angry about it, but I could see its impact on my relationships, especially with my family. I decided to do it for them because I could see how much it impacted them. Today, I will do it for myself. In addition, I see when my friends or clients have a problem that I might have seen as usual before because I was so accustomed to living with a chronic level of depression that I never thought that it was a problem in myself or others.

Today, I cannot believe I lived with such a profound level of depression for so long. I would NEVER live with that level of emotional pain today. Today, I know that was not normal. I am sad that no one could have helped me through that or that I hid it so well that I couldn't find help. I can see a future for myself in a way I never could.

I was going to write something filled with tips and techniques addressing self-care, but once I began to get REAL help for my mental health problems and accepted an adequate level of treatment, many of the issues I thought I had seemed to resolve themselves.

So, my final message is this: If you are chronically experiencing a level of discomfort, depression, or pain in your life, please get some help. And yes, you are probably going to have to take medication. Get over yourself. It could be so much worse. I asked my psychiatrist, in one final act, to rebel against taking medication, "What about all of the problems with big pharma?" She wisely responded, "Yes, big pharma is a problem, but you need to know that the science behind medicine is good, and it works."

Gus' parallel journey of addiction and mental illness

The first time I remember going to a counselor was in second or third grade. I had been nailing nails on the side of the house that my mom was renting because I was angry. I barely remember it. I remember it seemed odd; I did not understand why I was there or what was happening.

I frequently got in trouble in school but got good grades and many second chances. In high school, I found alcohol during my sophomore year. It helped me feel less afraid and act as I wanted. I got kicked off the track team for drinking on campus, got a drug and alcohol abuse counselor, and nearly missed my senior year and the cross-country team. We won the state championship, and I got to run at the end of the year because the teachers liked me.

My parents evicted me during my senior year in high school for a party I threw while my parents were in Hawaii. I did not know the house was in Escrow; luckily, the people buying it showed up. If they had shown up on the planned day, they would have seen a trashed yard and house. I was in a significant car accident during my senior year, and due to my severe neck injury, I was only able to attend three classes. I barely graduated.

Somehow, I made it into college at an excellent private school. In college, I struggled to get good grades and learn how to study. When I studied, I did very well. I was elevated to honor status, which allowed me access to special classes and teachers. I was getting straight A's, my research papers were getting the attention of my professors, and I was designing my unique major.

Then, I could not read or listen in class and was obsessed with my research. Despite everything I knew, I spoke up in class and explained everything the teacher taught. The students overreacted. One kid put his fingers to his head and pulled the trigger as if he had a gun.

The teacher asked, "Now that you have your theory, why don't you write your book?" After class, the teacher pulled me aside and asked if I was seeing a counselor or taking medication because I might need help.

She admitted to me that she took Prozac and that it helped her. I went to the university clinic and saw a psychiatrist who explained my symptoms and asked what it might be. She said it sounded like I might have bipolar disorder, and I asked her how I would know. She told me to take medication as prescribed for at least six months and see her every month.

I asked one of my friends to look after me. I started to lose track of the way I was feeling. I had these unforgettable moments with a girl, but I could not understand how I felt about her. So, I got drunk and tried to mess around with another girl to see how I felt. I started crying, and she asked what was wrong, and I said, "Sorry, I can't do this; it's wrong." I ran to the dorm room of the girl I was seeing and told her what I had done. She did not understand; it seemed ridiculous. I felt crazy; I was upset about what I had done, got very anxious, and tried to run away. My friend chased me. He saw that I wanted to jump off the building; he took all the medication I had, walked back to his room, and passed out.

When I woke up, I did not know how to speak and could not stand up. I was in the corner of the men's bathroom, and others asked me what was wrong, but I could not speak. The people called paramedics, and they placed me on a gurney. That was the first time I went to the hospital.

My parents came to pick me up for the summer, found a note on my dorm room door, went to the office, and learned I was in the hospital. When the hospital released me, my parents took me to their home.

I continued taking medication and seeing a doctor. My parents did not know what to do. I was triggered by being around them. One time, I felt crazy, told them to leave me alone, and backed away. My stepfather came at me, and I yelled at him to go away. But I flipped over a table, and he tackled me to the ground and started hitting me in the face. I was screaming for help. A neighbor overheard me and came running over, saw what was going on, and dropped an elbow on my stepfather's neck. He immediately let me go, and I went running through the woods.

The cops arrived later, two men and a woman. The woman cop told me my parents were crazy, and it was not safe for me to go home. They told me they would return the next day to get my stuff. The next day, the sheriff took me to my parents' house. My stepdad was yelling from the porch that I was weak for calling the cops.

I ended up leaving the area, found my biological father, tried to go back to school, and started raving and going out dancing all night. I found out my father was manufacturing methamphetamine, and I started using it. I ended up in San Francisco for a year, on many different drugs, until I finally lost my mind.

I took all the pills I could find and washed them down with cough syrup and alcohol. I held a phone to my head and went in and out of consciousness, debating on whether to call 911 because I could not afford the ambulance. I had trouble talking to my girlfriend and ended up at San Francisco State University Hospital on a psychiatric hold. They could not keep me because I had no insurance, so after a few days, I moved back in with my father and participated in manufacturing meth.

After many months, I could not remember when I was not high on drugs or drunk. I decided to try and stop. My head spun, and I could barely walk, afraid of not being high. For the first time in my life, I was addicted and not in control of my life anymore.

I got kicked out, and my girlfriend's family took me in. I got off the meth and stopped smoking weed, and thought I was doing well, just drinking. I got a job and a career, was successful, and started making money.

When my girlfriend broke up with me, I got severely depressed and could not eat or go to work; I ended up at Kaiser IOP (Intensive Outpatient) and got back on anti-depressants. I learned about CBT (Cognitive Behavioral Therapy) and started smoking pot. Pot, taking Prozac, and alcohol made me the life of the party until I started getting kicked out of bars.

A few months after the bouncers kicked me out of a bar, I returned, and they told me to get out. I stood up and tried to slam my beer. They grabbed my arms; I yelled and smashed my beer glass onto the bouncer's head. They held me down; the cops came, and my hand was bleeding a lot. I was yelling about my injuries, "Look what they did to me!" but I went to jail. I got bailed out after ten days and got a strike and a nine-month sentence. I was going to lose my job, my place to live, and my car, and I started calling my friends to have a "going to jail party." I moved in with my dad. I did not know he was still using drugs. Sometimes, he would hide his dope in liquid form. Unknowingly, I took a bottle of Gatorade full of dope, drank it, and felt very weird. I did not understand why, but then I remembered the taste in my mouth and realized there were drugs in the bottle. I no longer enjoyed that high. I felt horrible. I ended up at another bar, and the bouncers kicked me out. I punched out the plate glass window in front of the bar and took off running. I got tired fast. I turned the corner and rolled under a van, trying to hide from the people chasing me. I woke up hours later, my arm was sewn back up. A cop came in and told me he was on the scene where he found me, and he told me I was lucky to be alive. He had never seen that much blood on the ground except when someone died.

I went to jail. I called my mom from the payphone in the infirmary and told her what happened. She said, "I can't believe they found my son passed out under a car, bleeding to death." I could not get her voice out of my head, and it all became apparent.

I spent almost a year in jail, fighting my two strikes. I got into a dorm program and started learning about the disease of addiction, alcoholism, codependency, and a twelve-step program. I realized I could not continue drinking and using drugs and have a better life. Not being in my son's life was hard because I knew how it felt not to have my dad in my life. And I never wanted to do that to him. I was lucky. My public defender went to the same college as me and took a particular interest in my case. It got me in front of a judge who went to the same school and was likely to take away one of my strikes and only get probation and credit for time served.

I was in dual diagnosis drug court. I was required to go to a halfway house, attend a recovery program, outpatient, see my psychiatrist regularly, take medication, and go to meetings. I went to my first AA meeting out of jail, a large men's meeting. A member told me to find a sponsor who had what I wanted. I saw a well-dressed man who seemed to know what he was talking about. We worked the twelve steps together. I could start my own company, get off probation, start a record label, produce music, and publish books.

After a few years sober, I got married to a woman in the program. I found out I was severely depressed and non-responsive to medications. My doctor wanted me to go through electric shock treatments or a vagus nerve implant. We found out later that my depressive tendencies triggered her codependence, and she did not want to work it out, so we separated. I lost my job and medical insurance. I was unemployed for a while and without a doctor until I got my next job. I was doing well at work and took a year off dating after the divorce.

I met an artist/poet, and we had a tumultuous relationship. I started rapid cycling (going from extreme highs to extreme lows) multiple times a day and went to outpatient therapy. Luckily, the psychiatrist got my thyroid checked and believed that the thyroid was behind my mental health issues. I got it tested, and it was hyperactive.

I started having convulsions, shakes, and fainting spells. I called 911 on myself twice in two weeks to go to the emergency room before I found out the Lithium I was taking might have been at toxic levels. I went into the inpatient program, but I talked myself out of a two-week hold and went back to work too soon and lost my job.

I got severely depressed and tried to overdose on my meds. I woke up almost a week later, having been in a blackout for five days. I had been in the ER, and they transferred me to another psychiatric unit in another hospital.

When I got out, I started my own company again and finally moved back home. I hoped moving back home would get me closer to my family and son. The opposite was true. My siblings were not allowed to see me, and I wasn't allowed to see my son.

I went to court over custody. I got what I already had every other weekend, one night for dinner a week. I was living with my girlfriend and her three kids while I was able to support them for about a year. I was able to have my family experience with them. We broke up, and I had a young man I was sponsoring in the program relapse and die. Another friend tried to jump out of my car on the way to the psychiatric hospital.

After eight years of being clean and sober, I decided to drink again. I dislocated my shoulder while jumping off a bridge for fun.

My friend's mom had cancer, and she had fentanyl patches left over. She gave them to me, and I started taking them. I did not know how strong they were. I "came to" in bed one night. I knew I would not wake up again if I closed my eyes. I realized I was dying. I could not breathe and realized it was an opioid overdose. I pulled up my sleeve and had three patches on. I took two of them off and went back to AA.

I knew if I ever used drugs or alcohol again, I would overdose or crash a car drunk and kill myself or someone else. I realized I was a real alcoholic, but I thought I knew some people who smoked marijuana and seemed to manage OK, so I tried doing it alone. I ended up in the psychiatric hospital twice. I broke my hand teaching an old friend a "lesson." I got back on medication and tried to get sober, but I lost the will to live. I took all my medication, held the only picture of my ex-wife, and pleaded with God to take me.

When I woke up, I was angry to be alive. I knew I was a danger to myself and others if I were to drink and use, so I had to get sober but did not want to.

I traveled with a friend across the country, saw that my dad was doing better, and decided not to move back to where my family was.

I moved in with a college friend. We started dating, and I started doing heroin. One time, my son was visiting, and I completely blacked out. My girlfriend had to take him home. I swore I would never be under the influence in front of my son. She set a boundary and said she could not be in a relationship with someone doing what I was doing.

I got outpatient support and was active in AA. However, I was struggling to stay sober. I would get a few months, get loaded, and get a few months, I would get loaded. I got so fed up with early recovery and could not take it anymore.

Something changed. I felt connected to my supporting people and felt a part of the community again. Things seemed to be getting better as if I had a foothold in my life. I woke up one morning on a trip with my girlfriend and had several messages on my phone from my son's mom in the middle of the night. I knew something had happened to my son. He was in a car accident in critical condition.

Somehow, I knew he was already gone. We drove back home and spent a couple of days in the hospital with him before pulling the plug. My son was able to donate his organs. He was sixteen.

Life became simple. I would do what I needed to do each day to stay clean, sober, and alive, or I would die. I got a grief counselor who was familiar with addiction who had also lost her son in an accident. She helped me relate in a way that many people could not. I was numb from the shock but did what I needed to do each day. Sometimes, it meant watching TV and playing video games between support group meetings, exercising at the gym, taking my medication as prescribed, and seeing my doctor regularly. I had good support through the county in outpatient and started working with a new sponsor in AA. I learned to use ALL the tools that I learned over the years.

I have created a daily ritual: Each morning, I get up and write, list all the things I am grateful for, read a list of affirmations I have been writing since jail, read my meditation books, read some highlights in the book of Alcoholics Anonymous like acceptance and the daily reprieve and I pray and meditate. I exercise most days, and by the grace of God and the miracle of AA, my doctor and medication, and my support group, I can stay sober a day at a time since before my son passed over three years ago.

I have not had to go back to the hospital or suffer major depressive disorder since I have been sober again, even while grieving the loss of my son. A Higher Power graced me with recovery that has carried me through.

Dave, a veteran, shares his journey with his recovery from addiction, and through that process, he discovered he has PTSD and Major Depressive Disorder.

I never felt I belonged anywhere, not even with my own family, until the first time I took chemicals at age thirteen. They helped me feel as though I fit in, and they helped mask the feelings I had from being adopted.

I struggled in school from second grade through high school. Special education made me feel like an outcast. When I was using chemicals, it made me feel more normal, like others who were not in special ed.

It (taking chemicals) worked for two years until it was brought to my parent's attention by my special ed teacher that I appeared to be drunk or stoned in class. My parents sat me down and gave me an ultimatum: either go into a recovery program or move out. So, what is a fifteen-year-old supposed to do? I could not move out or get a job, so I went to rehab. I went through the motions, graduated, went to

AA meetings, and found the fellowship (social aspect), not the "program." I stayed clean and sober for three years.

At twenty-one, not knowing what to do with my life and having twin boys, I decided to join the Navy to give my sons something to be proud of me for. I was in the service for three years, not expecting to see war, but I spent nine months in the Persian Gulf during Desert Storm and Desert Shield. While in the Persian Gulf, we performed mine-sweeping operations to prepare for an amphibious assault. My ship was one of two to locate a mine. However, it exploded and ripped a 16 by 20-foot hole 10 feet away from me. It caused severe trauma, and the only relief I had was drinking alcohol. I continued this behavior for ten years afterward. I wound up getting in trouble twice while in the Navy to escape what I was feeling and removed from the service, which, to my relief, kept me from Somalia.

I got sober in 2000 because my behavior was going to land me in two places: prison or death. So, I entered the recovery rooms (AA & NA), and only this time did I find the program, not just the fellowship. After working the steps quite a few times and peeling the layers back, I realized why I drank and why my behavior had not changed. In one instance, I had a confrontation with a significant other via text that caused me to go over to her house. She indicated in her text that she did not want to live anymore; I had heard this several times before.

My intention when I got there was to show her what it looked like for someone to kill themselves. I showed up, knocked on her door, and she answered. There were some choice words. I put my knife to my wrist lengthwise, and I said, you keep saying that you do not want to be here anymore, and this is what it looks like. She called the police and said that I threatened to kill her when, in fact, that was not the case. They [police] came to my work, arrested me, took me to jail, and by some miracle, I managed to bail myself out.

At that point, I knew I needed to seek help and entered an anger management program. (There is a part of the big book of AA that states that we should seek outside professional help) so that's what I did, in two different ways: one through psychiatry and one through an organization called the Vet Center. After spending much time with the psychiatrist, he suggested medication, which I opposed because of my sobriety. He continued discussions until I was open-minded to taking something that was not mind-altering. After a few weeks, he came back to me with a medication that might work. At the time, studies had shown that anti-seizure medication helped those with PTSD. I agreed to start taking medication, and it helped and took the edge off stupidity in the world.

Between the program of AA, seeing my psychiatrist, and seeing someone at the Vet Center, I got the courage to go after the VA for service connection so they could help with my treatment. It took six years before I could even get my foot in the door for help because of my discharge, which was other than honorable because of my drinking, to get through the demons caused by the war. F***!

After finally being able to be seen at the VA, I was diagnosed with severe PTSD caused by combat with major depressive disorder. "Severe," which meant suicidal ideation and attempted suicide. Working with a psychologist and psychiatrist there and with my social worker and psychologist at the Vet Center, we began to formulate a recovery program that worked for me, which involved continued medication. I learned different ways to look at things and breathing techniques, a little thing called "five, four, three, two, one," which helped when my anxiety peaked.

I was watching TV and saw a program that provided service dogs to veterans with PTSD. I have always had dogs but didn't realize what they were doing (helping me cope with life), especially my dog Sienna. So, I started searching for a place to get one. I discovered a place in San Martin, CA, called Operation Freedom Paws. I submitted my application and prescription from my doctor and waited for the interview.

When I arrived, I was accepted and paired with a fantastic dog named Laddie. I thought he was only going to be for PTSD and anxiety, but these are amazing animals. Not only does he help me with anxiety and depression by keeping me in the present moment, but he is also very intuitive and alerts me to my pain level caused by injuries to my neck and back from being in the service. He helps with my mobility issues, which can be just getting up off the floor or getting dizzy from TBI (traumatic brain injury). He has even adapted and alerts me when he detects my cardiac issues.

The program also provides a psychologist on hand. After training, we do something called "Puppy yoga," which is not what you would think of as yoga. For us, it is a time when we sit down wherever it is comfortable, relax, and pay attention to our dogs. The onsite psychologist takes us through a breathing exercise and the "five, four, three, two, one." This is all designed so the dogs have a calm baseline.

I have used these techniques at concerts, Great America theme park, and getting through airports. I also use tapping, like a butterfly hug, which slows your breathing and heart rate. After certifying and regaining confidence, I was able to get certified as a peer support specialist so that I could help others find their way out of the darkness (depression). I gave up an eighteen-year career as a mechanic and went to work for Operation Freedom Paws to utilize all my experiences in dealing with PTSD, depression, and substance abuse, which helps our clients.

Becky Writes

My Adventures Through Hell: This essay is about how I'm creating comic strips to cope with PTSD. Yes, you heard me correctly - I'm making comic strips to cope with a mental health condition. I've done weirder things in my life.

What on earth is PTSD, you might ask? PTSD, or posttraumatic stress disorder, is a mental health diagnosis that applies to people who have been through a traumatic event (or multiple traumatic events) and experience several symptoms. They include persistent physiological arousal, including irritability, exaggerated startle response, and hypervigilance; changes in cognition and mood, including feelings of detachment from others, negative beliefs about oneself and the world, and inability to enjoy oneself; reexperiencing of the trauma, including intrusive memories, disturbing dreams, and flashbacks; and avoidance of reminders of the trauma. Yeah, I have all of those – I have all those, in spades. In spades, I tell you.

The thing that makes my PTSD extra special and tricky to deal with is that the trauma that created my PTSD is still ongoing. Heavens. I mean, seriously – like, this is my life? Really? Merciful Heavens. A one-time trauma is bad enough, but to have it keep on happening again and again. No, man – I wouldn't wish that on anybody.

But as I said above, I'm dealing with it – I'm dealing with it by making comic strips. I'm astonished because these comic strips are some of the most meaningful things I've done. Sometimes, it feels hard to reconcile the fact that something so magical came out of something truly awful: I'm simultaneously swimming in the sea of wonderfulness and terrible, horrible badness. The dreadful, horrible badness is what gave birth to the wonderfulness. Not only does that statement feel like a pile of contradictions that makes my poor brain feel confused, but there are so many intersections in the story I'm about to tell that it makes my head spin:

I'm dealing with both physical and psychological issues; I'm a psychologist with PTSD; I'm a psychologist who does art. I'm using art as a means of psychoanalysis and healing; this art looks at spiritual, psychological, and physical aspects of existence, and the self-analysis I'm engaging in is a collision between Carl Jung and Jacques Lacan. And as I said above, this art is an intersection between the beautiful and the horrific.

Let's look at Intersection Number One: I'm a psychologist who treats people with mental disorders, and I have one myself (not that it's uncommon, but there it is). It has tripped me out, from time to time, to be sitting with clients and hear their PTSD narratives – to hear narratives that sound just like mine. I must bite my tongue not to say, "That happens to me, too!!!!" I must bite my tongue to not make the session about me.

See, I have a PTSD diagnosis from another psychologist I'm seeing. I trust her judgment because she's a smart cookie – she works at the VA, where they deal with much of that stuff. I'm also seeing a psychoanalyst with whom I've been working for many years. Why two therapists, you might ask? This one doctor-guy who works in the same building I work in said, "You'd better see this old colleague of mine because she's a good CBT therapist," those CBT therapists tend to be good at managing a crisis as it comes along. And it came along.

In October 2019, I came down with a health condition that brought me to my knees. Before it started, I was a fully functioning, ordinary human being, getting through life and having an ordinary time. My life was neither good nor bad. It was so-so. Well, no. That's total and complete hogwash. Before this thing started, my life was Heaven. My life was absolute Heaven, but I had no idea it was that until that day: The horrible, awful, lousy day.

It was October 20th, or thereabouts, in 2019, and I was chilling in front of my favorite movie. I completed work that week, and it was time to relax and not think about anything. Then I heard this sound in my right ear. It felt and sounded to me like some muscle spasm. It was like the hum of machinery sounds, a low-pitched flutter. I thought, "Okay, that's odd" and peculiar. But I figured it was just some one-time thing, just some weird oddity that the body does occasionally. But no. It happened again about a minute later. I thought, "This isn't good," but hopefully, it'll pass. It did pass after about a half hour of hearing those dumb sounds every minute or so. The funny thing is, I totally and completely forgot that it had ever happened after it went away. I totally and completely forgot until two days later, it happened again. "Well, crap", I thought. But the good thing was my work week was over in about a half hour.

Again, I totally and completely forgot about the whole thing until a week later. This time, it happened on a Sunday night, and it lasted about three or four hours. Then, it was gone until the following Wednesday night, when it kept me up for six hours. In this case, the sounds had gotten so deafeningly loud that they sounded like a sub-woofer at a rock concert—but the messed-up thing was that it was inside my ear! There was no way to get away from it!

Well, I won't go into the details of every episode I experienced because there were many of them. They were the worst torture of my life. I'm already susceptible to noise – for example, music and TV sounds from neighbors' apartments are painful. I'm that sensitive. So, you can imagine how horrible it must've been for me, a sensitive soul, to have these noises go on for hours and hours at a time – and have no way to get away from them.

I saw doctor after doctor, who dismissed my symptoms as tinnitus, and they all had the helpful recommendation of: "Get used to it." None of them believed it was muscular, even though every fiber of my being knew that it was. Maybe medical schools don't do an excellent job teaching ear anatomy. These doctors do not know that muscles in the ear can spasm like any other muscle.

I had to do my web research to figure out my condition, and I discovered a diagnosis that sounded spot on: Middle Ear Myoclonus. These two muscles in the middle ear can go into spasm and create sounds just like what I described. After figuring out what I had, I did a Google search: "Ear Doctor LA Middle Ear Myoclonus," that's how I found the physician who confirmed my diagnosis. He made some brilliant suggestions and a treatment plan, the last resort of which is surgery, where he cuts the offending muscles. He gave me some muscle relaxers, which helped take the edge off but didn't make the problem go away entirely.

Then another good thing happened: from April to mid-August, I had a remission from this condition. It's gotten a little hairier recently, but it's not nearly as bad as it was at its onset (fingers crossed it stays that way until I can get going with the rest of my doctor's treatment plan, which is delayed by all the COVID stuff).

Anyway, what has this got to do with coping with mental and emotional problems? Middle Ear Myoclonus is a physical thing, you all are thinking. Yeah, you got a point there. I'm talking about this awful horribleness because that's what landed me with the PTSD diagnosis – let me unpack that just a bit. Posttraumatic Stress Disorder is a funny little diagnosis because it's different from all the other ones. In the case of depression and anxiety and all that, you look at the symptoms the person is experiencing to arrive at a diagnosis, but you don't look at the cause. PTSD is different because you look at the cause; that's what Criterion A is about.

Criterion A is where you must be exposed to an event that causes trauma. It must be one of four things:

- It's either life-threatening or something

where you think your life is in danger.

- You get seriously injured.

- You are a victim of sexual violence.

- You witness (either directly or indirectly) one of these things happening to someone else.

Now, most of you might think, yeah, ear noises are not a serious injury, sexual trauma, or life-threatening. They're just noises. Many people even told me, "At least your condition is not life-threatening." But it WAS.

Let me unpack that a bit. The constant torture every couple of days or so was destroying me. Those ear noises tortured me, or I continually dreaded and anticipated their return. When the noises happened, it felt like an electric shock – my entire body jolted by electricity. Every single nerve in my body would explode from its shock. I was literally one of those lab animals being shocked repeatedly to see how many shocks would eventually destroy that poor animal psychologically. And the thing is, as much as people were trying to be helpful, saying it wasn't life-threatening, it was the worst thing you could have possibly said to me. I wished it was life-threatening because being dead would have ended the pain. I thought of taking my life many, many times. That's why my two competent therapists agree that I have PTSD for real – because there were times when my life was literally in danger. I met criterion A with flying colors.

And what about the other criteria? Here's how those came about – you hear about it with soldiers who come back from war with PTSD – they keep their life together while they're on active duty, but as soon as they come home, they fall apart. That very same thing happened to me during the period of remission I told you about. Before that, I was trying to survive each day in a constant state of terror. I was working and functioning like an ordinary human being – most people who looked at me wouldn't even know something was wrong. But, inside, I was like those soldiers on the battlefield – just trying to keep myself together.

Then, the flashbacks and intrusive memories started after things quieted down in April 2020.

I'd be going about my day and then suddenly feel like it was December 2019 again (the worst month of my life). I had to concretely tell myself, "No, this is a different time. It's now July 2020". I started having dreams about the icky ear sounds coming back. Some days, I'd swim in memory soup so deep that I thought I'd drown. My startled response was (and still is) off the charts. Any little unexpected sound and I jump out of my skin – it probably doesn't help that the nature of my trauma was actual bad sounds. The list goes on and on. I've had to fight like a dog to keep myself grounded in the present. Good Lord, Lucy.

Dang, where does the coping come in amidst all that? Yeah. I honestly and sincerely believe that making this awful torture into art is, at least in part, what saved my life. Even though I've been in a constant state of terror, making meaning out of all this has been one of the most important things I've done in my life. Here's how it started:

Last January (January 2020), I met up with this Jungian consultation group I belonged to. I told them how bad the ear condition was and how much it was ruining my life. We all cried together. One said, "Hey, why don't you try doing some active imagination?" Active imagination is a Jungian technique where you take something from your psyche – say, an image that popped up in a dream, a symptom, or a symbol - something along those lines – and have a dialogue with your unconscious about it. You have a dialogue to see if you can get insight into problems affecting your life. That group member, she was all, "Why don't you take your graphic novel characters and have you and them jump into your ear and see if you can get any ideas about why this symptom is knocking at your door?" At that point, I knew these characters well because I'd done four graphic novels and a couple of comic books. I could trust them to go on an adventure with me inside my ear.

So, that's what I did. My two graphic novel characters and I jumped into my right ear and ended up in this freaky hellscape. It was a dark place, and we met up with some scary figures, the stuff of which nightmares are made. In this land of awfulness, we looked around for anything that might give us clues as to why this horrible symptom was knocking at my door. Is my body trying to tell me something? Is my psyche trying to tell me something and using my stupid ear to communicate it? It was worth trying to see. In any event, I figured it wouldn't do any harm.

Sometimes, I'll start drawing the comic strip and see what comes out, and other times, I'll do some automatic writing first that takes the form of dialogues with figures in my unconscious – after that, I find a way to translate it into comic strip form. The outcome of this process is something Dali-esque at times. At the same time, I've always admired Surrealism and incorporated it into my art; this is the most surreal material I've created. And the beautiful part is – I wasn't even trying to be surreal. It was all organic.

About a month into doing this, I started showing the art to my analyst. It became clear to me that the content I was generating was a waking dream, and we started analyzing the content as if it were a dream – In the Lacanian style. Some wackadoodle insights have come out of that analysis. The fact that these comics were inspired by Jung but subjected to Lacanian analysis makes for a fantastic, intersectional form of therapeutic work, as I stated above.

After I'd done enough of these comics, I decided to make them into actual comic books: The first three books are about me and my graphic novel characters going through those hellscapes, getting insight here and there about my symptoms, my life, and all that. In the following four books, the characters get transported out of Hell and into the regular world – something unexpected. Still, my unconscious told me those characters had to return to ordinary reality. We could analyze me and my life more deeply in that state of ordinariness. My unconscious was talking to us through a 1970s-style TV as we sat on a couch in a living room.

What have I learned? I've learned all kinds of cool stuff about the nature of reality – that old unconscious of mine is a smart cookie when it comes to all that. It's teaching me not to fear death, as well, and it led me to do some fascinating work with ancestral trauma. The comic work bled into the music I make and inspired two albums, one of which I'm still working on.

Interestingly, in April of 2020, when COVID was starting, one of the comic strips told me to go to my parents' house (in a roundabout way). My therapists agreed with what the comics were saying, so I went up there to shelter in place for COVID. Oddly and unexpectedly, that temporary move did make my symptoms go into remission for several months. Apparently, middle ear myoclonus is heavily impacted by one's emotional state, and being with family has helped a lot. Maybe I'm just reaching, but I'm getting the strong impression that that old unconscious of mine wanted me to go up north because it knew that a temporary move would improve my symptoms. Thanks for that!!!

A few months ago, one of the comic characters (an owl who used to be a cassette tape) told me I would have to get ear surgery. At the time, I was perplexed because my ears weren't doing so poorly. But now that things are not great, I realize the owl was probably right. I have one more medication I'm going to try before I make the leap and go under the knife. But the old owl is correct, and no medicine on the planet will fix this. Interestingly, keeping busy and focusing on things (like the comics and this writing I'm doing) also keeps the ear noises away.

So, even though the comics were intended to give me some insight into my symptoms, they are also helping me to control it. Additionally, when I'm focusing on the comics, my PTSD symptoms quiet down – the flashbacks and terror take a backseat to the creative process. Another unexpected discovery I made was that making these comics is helping to reprocess the trauma itself. Writing about the awful ear stuff, as well as some other traumatic events in my past, had the same impact on me as an EMDR session (EMDR is Eye Movement Desensitization Reprocessing Therapy – it is an evidence-based trauma treatment that is powerfully effective).

As I considered publishing these comic books as a seven-volume set, I started researching publishers. I stumbled upon a website that stated that DARPA (Defense Advanced Research Projects Agency) is researching using comics as trauma therapy. Man, I thought. I reinvented the wheel that someone had already invented – but accidentally.

Finally, of super-major importance is the fact that these comics helped reconnect me with my spirituality. What happened to me destroyed my whole belief system and any connections whatsoever with what used to be my spirituality. It made me believe in Hell because now I've been there. It made me question whether God even exists. It made me feel completely isolated, alone, unprotected, and forgotten by an indifferent universe. Talking to the animals and people unconsciously reminded me of who I am again and connected me with the divine in ways I'd never experienced.

I'll include an excerpt for you all to see. I redid a new version of this book to fit onto the page (I use 8.5 x 11 size paper for this project). So, that's my adventure through Hell – the name of the comic book series is *Hell*. I'm hoping the day will come when this ear condition is in my rearview mirror and I can get past this PTSD. But, in the meantime, some good art is coming out of it – today, I drew the 300th page.

Chapter 5

Poetry & Quotes

"Acceptance is Key"

Post-Traumatic Stress is still with me,
Awareness is the key.
To keep my serenity,
Sometimes, I feel insanity.

Create different dreams,
That before could not be seen.
A new reality
I can now see.

Hope is real- It helps to heal.
All the beauty
In the most minor things.

Experience shows,
That I know

How to grow.
Help others with their woes.

Never-ending journey:
Become a survivor.
Become a warrior.
Love is armor.

Protects from harm,
It can weather the storm.
Feelings run deep,
Good memories to keep.

Follow your bliss,
Give yourself a kiss.
Respect who you are:
-A magnificent star

Become reborn,
Through the worst storm.
Smiles and laughter,
Your biggest treasures.

Share the wealth,
Of renewed health.
The one thing worth knowing:
Is "Happiness is Being"

"Ongoing Process"

Continued healing
Occasionally grieving
Of innocence lost
At a high cost

Too young to know,
If intentions are real
Until it's too late
And I can't escape.

Cut off from friends,
Isolation begins.
Final blow
So, I had to go.

I needed a plan,
To leave that man.
Help from others,
To recover.

It took many years,
To shed tears.
Lots of therapy,
And the help of Reiki.

Ward off despair,
That was always there.

Flashbacks still happen,
But not as often.

Becoming aware,
Of what was there.
"This is a memory,
Inside of me".

What I must
Is trust.
Breathe deep,
Sanity keeps.

Laugh or cry,
Doesn't matter why.
Feeling Is healing.

Forgive-move on,
Becoming strong.
Smile and play,
Every day.

Controlled no more,
Free to explore.
Dreams come true,
Visions come through.

Make a list,
Choose happiness.

Finally free,
To be me.

"Progress"

Moving forward into a better condition. Isn't that what life's all about?

Spiritually, mentally, and emotionally. Recovering and growing from the pain, becoming a softer human being, improving one's outlook on the world, and bringing love and compassion to others. There are no world wars, just inner violence within one's community. How does a person set a positive example? Patience and tolerance towards others, forgiveness with the spirit of love, helping one another through our pain, and giving without expecting anything in return. Joyfulness and gratitude for life. From anger, hostility, and vengefulness to forgiveness, understanding, and compassion, the realization of a sacred life. The gift of being human- not something we awaken to for many years. Is there always room for progress? Of course, there is – every day:

Could I have been more patient in traffic? Could I have smiled at someone in the grocery store? Could I have made someone's day by letting them go first? Yes, there is always room to move forward to a better condition. It's called progress. And I thank my Higher Power for the opportunity to improve.

Coventina Waterhawk's Quotes:

"We can start over at any time. Now is the perfect time.

"Everything is in Divine order."

"Happiness is Being."

"Feeling is Healing."

"Gratitude flows out of me like a rushing waterfall."

"I am serene like a stilled pond."

"I go with the ebb and flow of my life's experiences."

"Being gentle with ourselves while experiencing a PTSD flashback is a form of self-love."

"Forgiveness makes our hearts lighter."

"HOPE: **H**elping **O**thers **P**rocess **E**motions"

Resources

National Suicide Prevention Lifeline at 1-800-273-8255 or 9-8-8. You will be connected to a skilled, trained counselor at a crisis center in your area. This service is available 24/7. http://www.suicidepreventionlifeline.org/

SAMHSA National Helpline at 1-800-622-4357 | SAMHSA's National Helpline is a free, confidential, 24/7, 365-day-a-year treatment referral and information service for individuals and families facing mental health and/or substance use disorders. Services are available in English and Spanish. www.samhsa.gov/find-help/national-helpline

NAMI National Alliance for Mental Illness: 1-800-950-6264 Nami.org

Alcoholics Anonymous: www.aa.org (212) 870-3400

Al-Anon Family Groups: (Family & friends of Alcoholics) https://al-anon.org

Narcotics Anonymous: www.usa-na.org

Nar-Anon: (Family & friends of Addicts) https://www.nar-anon.org/

U.S. Veterans Crisis Line at 1-800-273-8255 (Press 1): The Veterans Crisis Line connects Veterans in crisis and their families and friends with qualified, caring Department of Veterans Affairs responders through a confidential, toll-free hotline, online chat, or text. Veterans and their loved ones can call or text 741741 to receive confidential support 24 hours a day, seven days a week, 365 days a year. https://www.veteranscrisisline.net/

Call Your Local Resources | Many cities in the U .S. and Canada have special local numbers, such as 21-1, to connect you with non-emergency organizations that provide health and human services assistance. Local centers often have additional language options if you want to speak a language other than English.

Videos, Books, & Additional Resources

Behavioral Tech offers videos and books intended for clients and families. Find a DBT group in your area:
www.psychologytoday.com/us/groups/dialect ical-dbt

Videos for Clients and Families:

Here are videos we recommend for clients and families:

• *From Chaos to Freedom: vimeo.com/ondem and/dbtskills*

- *Opposite Action: Changing Emotions You Want to Change*: *vimeo.com/ondemand/dbtskills*

- *If Only We Had Known: A Family Guide to Borderline Personality Disorder*: www.borderlinepersonalitydisorder.org/video -series

- *DBT Addiction Skills*: wewantrelief.com/therapy/dbt-for-substance -abuse (508) 715-8224

National Eating Disorders Information:

1-800-931-2237

bulimia.com/eating-disorders/eating-disorder -hotlines/

American Foundation for Suicide Prevention:
Toll-Free: 1-888-333-AFSP (2377)

Transgender Suicide Hotline:

1-877-565-8860

Hotline that is staffed entirely by transgender people to serve transgender people.

Depression and Bipolar Support Alliance (DBSA)-find a support group in your area:

Toll-free: (800) 826-3632

https://www.dbsalliance.org/

Anxiety and Depression Association of America

(ADAA) https://adaa.org/

Anorexia Nervosa and Associated Disorders (ANAD)

Hotline: 1-630-577-1130

National Mental Health Association

Helpline: 1-800-969-6642

PTSD support groups:

https://ptsd.supportgroups.com/

PSI: Postpartum Support International:

1-800-944-4773

https://www.postpartum.net/get-help/locations/

Schizophrenia Alliance:

1-800-493-2094

https://www.sardaa.org/

Multiple Personality Disorder: Psych Central: A multitude of references for mental health issues.

https://psychcentral.com/resources/Dissociation/SupportGroups/

American Psychiatric Association. (2013). *Diagnostic and Statistical Manual of Mental Disorders* (5th ed.).

If you read one book by Carl Jung, the following is recommended: Jung, C.G. (1963). *Memories, Dreams, Reflections.*(A. Jaffee,Ed.). London: Fortuna Press.

To learn more about active imagination, see: Johnson, Robert A. (1986). *InnerWork: Using Dreams and Active Imagination for Personal Growth*. New York: HarperCollins.

Here's a book about Lacanian Psychoanalysis: Fink, B. (1999). *A Clinical Introduction to Lacanian Psychoanalysis: Theory and Technique*. USA: First Harvard University Press.

To learn more about EMDR therapy, you can read this: Shapiro, F. (2012). *Getting Past Your Past: Take Control of Your Life with Self-help Techniques from EMDR Therapy*. Emmaus, PA:Rodale Books.

About the Author

Coventina Waterhawk is a testament to the transformative power of resilience, redemption, and self-discovery. As a child, she possessed an innate intuition, but the weight of mental illness and substance use challenges overshadowed this gift. Despite the darkness that clouded her path, Coventina persevered, embarking on a journey of healing and self-reclamation. Through the arduous recovery journey, Coventina found stability and unearthed her dormant intuitive abilities.

Today, she stands as an embodiment of hope and healing, channeling her intuitive gifts to facilitate balance and transformation in the lives of others. In addition to her role as an energy healer, Coventina is a passionate advocate for mental health awareness and addiction recovery. She has been a dynamic motivational speaker, speaking to large and small groups and sober since September 1986. The very first time she shared her experiences with others was in a psychiatric hospital after only seven days sober. Speaking has been her favorite way to serve her community. She believes in the power of holistic healing, integrating her personal experiences with professional expertise to offer guidance and support to those in need.

Beyond her professional endeavors, Coventina has created a women's spirituality circle to unite women from diverse spiritual backgrounds to celebrate seasonal holidays, focusing on personal growth and healing. She enjoys being entertained by her fur babies, Jezebel and Cinnamon. She recently moved from the hustle and bustle of Silicon Valley to a slower-paced life in New Mexico. Coventina continues to inspire change, foster compassion, and empower individuals on their journey toward wholeness and self-discovery.